M000301002

If It's Thursday
I Can't Hear You

Rex John

Copyright © 2018 Rex John

The moral right of the author has been asserted.

All characters and events in this publication, other than those clearly in the public domain, are fictitious and any resemblance to real persons, living or dead, is purely coincidental.

All rights reserved.

No part of this publication may be reproduced, stored in a retrieval system, or transmitted, in any form or by any means, without the prior permission in writing of the copyright holder, nor be otherwise circulated in any form of binding or cover other than that in which it is published and without a similar condition including this condition being imposed on the subsequent purchaser. For information address the author at raj@rexjohn.com

ISBN-13: 978-0-9884964-2-2
ISBN-10: 0-9884964-2-9

Author's Note

Who needs a laugh? I have been working on this book off and on for the past three years. As with everything else in my life, I got interested, then I lost interest, then I got interested again, etc., etc. Rinse and repeat. But now it is the end of 2018, and if you happen to be reading this book during the next year or so, well, you know full well why we all need a laugh these days.

If on the other hand, this book stands the test of time and you aren't reading it until, say, the year 2020 or beyond, you may have forgotten what turbulent times we were living in back in 2017 and 2018. Suffice it to say, a lot of people were angry and unhappy.

But times change, and I hope they will again. Meanwhile, perhaps this silly book will give you an occasional grin or giggle. I hope so.

Here is a suggestion I received from a reader not long ago. He wrote, "Mr. John, I hope you won't be insulted, but I put your book in the bathroom and read one story each day. When I finish, I just start over again."

I wrote back, "Insulted? Heavens no. You're reading my book, and that makes me happy. Besides, when an author has the last name 'John' and plasters his name all over the cover, he shouldn't be at all surprised that some of his books end up there."

So, wherever you happen to be reading this book, my only hope is that you will find it enjoyable.

Happy reading!

Rex John

Table of Contents

If It's Thursday I Can't Hear You

The Torture Museum

Several years ago we spent the better part of a month in Prague, Czech Republic. After a four-hour train ride from Vienna we made our way to the nearest ATM to withdraw cash in Czech Korunas — not to be confused with Mexican Coronas which would cost approximately 60,000 Czech Korunas — each.

As the money came shooting out of the ATM — I wish you could see Brad's face when this happens; it is something to behold — a strange person appeared out of nowhere and frantically started telling us he could "change it for us."

Our driver told us later we did the right thing when we politely declined his offer. Apparently the guy's speciality is "changing" the money from your hands to his.

We had used VRBO.com to rent a two bedroom apartment, and it was ideally located right in the middle of town. We could easily walk anywhere we wanted to go.

The apartment itself was okay, but nothing to write home about. It had two-feet thick walls (seriously!) and featured a TV with a couple of U.S. channels, a dishwasher just like the one we have at home, a double-sink bathroom, a tub with a handheld shower and a washer and dryer.

The building, according to our landlord, was built during the Gothic era — most likely in the 1400s. Who knew they had dishwashers back then!

The biggest oddity was that there was a slight elevation change between each room — only an inch or so, but enough that we tripped from room to room during our entire stay. The other strange thing was that the curtains in every room didn't fully cover the windows — they left a full twelve-inch gap right down the center, which meant our neighbors were in for a real treat! (If you define "treat" as watching two old guys sit at their computers when they're not taking naps.)

We enjoy all of our adventures, but Prague holds some special memories as we spent virtually every day exploring and just wandering the streets. The only near mishap we had was when I dared to take a photo of the *sign* on the outside of the American Embassy. A guard ran up to me and told me in no uncertain terms that photography was not allowed! I was tempted to say, "And you call this America!?!" but I decided against it.

Prague has numerous museums and concert halls and we made a serious effort to see as many as we could. One memorable visit was to the Communism Museum which was about the tackiest place I've ever been. My six year-old granddaughter could do better displays.

According to a mimeographed pamphlet we were given at the entrance, the museum gave insight into everyday life during Communist era in Czechoslovakia: politics, history, sports, economics, education, art, propaganda, the People's Militias, the army, the police (including the secret police), censorship, and courts and other institutions of repression, including show trials and political labor camps during the Stalinist era.

Tacky or not, it was fascinating and we read *every single word* in *every single display*.

Save yourself a trip.

Here's the bottom line: Communism=Bad.

We considered a trip to The Torture Museum, but after the Communism Museum we were afraid it would seem like overkill.

So we got a massage instead.

I am a big believer in *Trip Advisor*, and I should blush as I tell you that I am a "Level 6" reviewer (with 70,000 readers!) which I assume is similar to having a black belt in karate. So after a careful TripAdvisor search, we settled on a place with glowing reviews called "Thai Massage."

At this point I will mention, for the record, that Brad detests massages almost as much as I love them. There, I've said it. Now, let's continue....

"Thai Massage" — that's the name as well as a description of the business — was located on the third floor of an old building just off Old Town Square which is where they used to torture and behead people by massaging them to death.

No, just kidding, Brad!

By the time we climbed to the third floor I can tell you I was ready for a leg massage.

We were greeted by a cordial receptionist and...*what is that smell!?* I honestly don't know how to describe it. It was an odor that would put hair on your chest. At first I thought it was the smell of curry, but then I decided it was boiled cabbage. Then I decided it was boiled cabbage with curry. Finally I realized it was just old gym socks — probably in the pot with the curry and the boiling cabbage. I spent the first 89 minutes of our 90-minute massage trying to suppress my gag reflex.

Thai massage, as you may know, involves keeping your clothes on, which is a decided plus for people who are not looking for a "happy ending." In this joint, however, we were told to change into clothes provided for the customers to wear: a prison-orange colored shirt and Hawaiian board shorts. The net effect was that we looked like Tibetan monks on holiday.

We were shown into a curtained cubicle with two mats on the floor. There was a curtain between the mats, too, but it remained open. As a result, our two female massage "therapists" were able to talk to each other non-stop in Chinese, or Thai, or Czech, or a combination of all three.

Non-stop. For ninety minutes.

I told Brad afterward that I thought they were talking about us, but he said I was being paranoid. But it was either that or they were trading recipes for Thai Curry Gym Sock Cabbage Soup.

To say my massage felt like torture is to understate how much it hurt. It wasn't just the pounding and punching — that was no worse than having somebody beat me up with a baseball bat. No, it was the twisting of my limbs into places and shapes they'd never been before. At one point I realized she had managed to bend my arm in a way I'd never seen. I wasn't sure if she'd broken it or that we'd just discovered that I was double-jointed. Either way, I was in agony.

I had a small bit of revenge when she climbed on top of me to take a little walk on my back. I am, shall we say, somewhat "rotund," so when I am lying face-down on the floor I look like an upside down turtle, which makes for difficult walking as I roll from side-to-side — so of course she fell off. I laughed aloud when I realized what had happened, which was good because it caused my neck to pop back into place.

Brad, on the other hand — you know, the guy who hates massage — seemed to love his. I'm so glad because I plan to demonstrate some of those same moves on him just as soon as I finish making him a new soup recipe I found.

My Life as a Great Inventor

If you read my book *The Pillow Goes Under Your Head*, you know Brad is as close to perfect as a person can get.

But like most people, he does have a flaw or two — one of which will probably make people question his sanity if I ever decide to make them public which, of course, I am about to do.

The man has a thing for vacuum cleaners.

Okay, that's fairly innocent as fetishes go, but let's face it — it's still weird.

We had at one time no fewer than six — count 'em, *six!* — working vacuum cleaners.

I first noticed his affliction when I started falling over the machines placed strategically around the house. We lived in a four-story condominium at the time, and on the days when our housekeeper was due I noticed that he placed a vacuum in the middle of each floor.

"What are you doing?" I asked the first time I saw him wheel one of the machines into the center of the living room and walk away.

"Putting the vacuum cleaner out so Gretchen can find it," he said.

"Because you don't think she's smart enough to open the hall closet to look for it?"

Then I went up a floor to the bedrooms and found another one in the middle of the hallway. The same on the fourth floor, where we watched television and had a small outdoor deck. Another vacuum. Down on the ground floor (garage and workroom) yet another. I didn't know if I should call someone to report this odd behavior or wait on the porch to forewarn the housekeeper that she was about to enter Crazy Town.

I will admit that this may bother me a bit more than it should because I, too, have something of a...um... *history* with vacuum cleaners.

When I was in junior high school, my stepmother bought a new, top-of-the-line, state-of-the-art, expensive — did I say expensive — vacuum cleaner, which I promptly dubbed The Big Sucker. (When my dad found out what she had paid, he applied the name to her.) She pretended that she bought it for herself, but it wasn't long till she started holding Vacuum Cleaner Classes and guess who was the only student?

After reviewing each of the attachments (there were about forty as I recall) with a demonstration of how each was to be used, she moved on to the ultra-long automatically retracting cord.

"Just make sure you don't run over this cord like your cousin Melvin did," she admonished. "He cut his mother's cord completely in half!" I decided to ignore the obvious Freudian implications of her statement and we moved on.

But her statement did raise a few questions, mostly having to do with (a) why Cousin Melvin had never told me he was an idiot; and (b) how the hell a vacuum cleaner could cut an electrical cord in half. Did it have a *blade* in there? Could it double as a lawn mower?

The final lesson was a demonstration of how the hose could be removed from one side and attached to the other, effectively turning something that sucked into something that blew.

And yes, I mean that in every sense of the word.

"Why?" I asked, sounding as dumb as Melvin. "Are you saying we just vacuum stuff up and then blow it back out?"

"No," she answered patiently, as if talking to a dimwit. "It's so you can gently blow the dust off fragile surfaces like the leaves of plants and the draperies."

And that, friends, became the impetus for the Birth of My First Great Invention.

It wasn't long after the vacuum purchase that the very same Stepmother (who was clearly trying to add "Wicked" to her moniker) called me from her downtown office one afternoon shortly after I had arrived home from school.

"What are your plans for the next two hours?" she wanted to know.

"Nothing. I'm going to go hang out with Lance (the kid next door)."

"No you're not. I want you to rake the front lawn."

"Rake?" I asked in a voice that implied she'd just asked me to plant a field of alfalfa.

"Yes, and I will expect it to be done by the time I get home." *Click.*

As I hung up the phone I looked out the window at the expanse of lawn which was now covered in leaves, two or three feet deep by my estimation. I could already feel the blisters starting to form on my hands from all the raking I was about to do.

Fortunately (or unfortunately, depending on your perspective — that is, whether you are a working mother or a smart-ass junior high kid) I had to pass the linen closet on the way to the garage and that's where The Big Sucker was kept.

Why rake the lawn when I could vacuum it!?

I hauled that monster out onto the front lawn, unreeled its retractable cord as far as it would reach (which wasn't far enough, so I fetched an extension cord) and flipped the switch!

It worked brilliantly! In fact, I had cleaned up two or three square feet before it started making ugly noises and I had to shut it off.

Hmmm, I thought, at this rate it should only take about 700 vacuum cleaner bags before this lawn is spic-n-span!

But we had only one spare bag, which is when the proverbial lightbulb went off over my head and I remembered this monster also could blow!

I quickly reversed the hose and away I went!

Unfortunately, it wasn't all that powerful and it would be years before somebody else stole my idea and made the modern day leaf blower. Ironically, I'd forgotten all about my own "invention" until years later when my mother-in-law gave me a leaf blower for Christmas. Nobody had ever heard of a "leaf blower" up until then (except me, of course, and I'd forgotten) so naturally I plugged it in and managed to blow most of the ornaments off the tree.

But I digress.

Recalling this misadventure has caused me to wonder

how many modern day inventions have been inspired by everyday appliances.

For example, I recently saw a TV commercial for a battery-operated "Body Scrubber" which supposedly exfoliates the dead skin from your body while you're in the shower. (I know: ewww!) But when I saw the demonstration, it reminded me of my dad's electric sander. I wonder if he ever thought about hauling that thing into the shower with him and scrubbing his dead skin off? If he had, he might have been known as the inventor of the Great Body Scrubber instead of just a building contractor.

And have you ever paid attention to the action of your windshield wipers? Back and forth they go, scraping all the bugs and bug poop off your window leaving it shiny clean. What if you invented something that did the same thing to your teeth!? (Not that I'm suggesting you have bugs and bug poop on your teeth.) Wouldn't that be wonderful? Well, guess what — I'll bet somebody paid attention to their windshield washers and when they got home they ran right into their house and invented the electric toothbrush! Eureka!

For a while one of our many vacuum cleaners was a Roomba, the nifty little robot that cleans your floors while you are away. (It also throws itself down the stairs committing vacuum suicide, but that's another story.) I'd bet money that the Roomba idea came to some guy who was watching his kid's battery-operated toy scooting all over the floor and thought, "Too bad that thing doesn't have a vacuum cleaner attached to it!"

The list is endless, and chances are that if you really start paying attention you too can invent something just like I did! And maybe your invention will suck too!

We Can't Play the Piano and Don't Want to Learn

As I write this I am seated on the deck of a cottage we have rented for the month of July in Sebastopol, California. The cottage is tucked behind a bigger house which faces the street, and while we share a roof, the living spaces are entirely separate.

The owner lives in the front of the house and at first we wondered if this would be a problem. Would she knock on our door every morning to see if "things were alright"? Would she check to make sure our bed was made, or the dishes done?

As it turns out, we needn't have worried. Carol is one of the kindest, sweetest people we've ever met and honestly, if she decides to stop by every day we wouldn't mind in the least. Instead, she never says a word to us unless we say something first. She often walks right by our front porch on her way to the garden without even looking at us. That's how determined she is not to be "in the way."

We love this place. It is bright and clean and airy, surrounded by huge trees and bountiful plants. I am seated under a red umbrella — just as I would be on our own patio at home — watching as the leaves in the big trees all around me sway gently in the breeze. It is a perfectly comfortable 72 degrees here (I just checked — it's 120 degrees at home). It is as perfect a day as one could imagine — the kind of lazy summer day that takes us back to our youth.

In fact, somewhere — a few houses away — I can hear a piano being played, just as it might have been in the neighborhood of my youth. Somebody is practicing the piano. Probably some young prodigy, with a helicopter mom standing over him or her with a big stick, waiting to beat him if he misses a note.

I wish that had been my mom! I laughingly tell my friends that I wish my parents had beaten me to make me practice the piano when I was a child, but of course I don't mean it. I wish they'd wheeled the piano out to the front yard and set it on fire.

It was my grandmother who wanted me to take piano lessons, so piano lessons I did take. One of her church lady friends, Mrs. Stull, showed up once a week to torture me, for which she collected three dollars.

My grandmother called Mrs. Stull "Brownie" for no reason apparent to me, and she was in her early 90s by my estimate, although in retrospect she was probably just 40 or so. She was thoroughly coiffed and powdered, emitting a smell of roses or lilac, or both. My grandmother kept both flavors of bathroom spray in our bathroom, and I have a hunch she may have thought it was perfume.

Her mousy brown hair was pulled into a neat bun at the nape of her neck, and she had little wire glasses perched on the end of her pointed nose. The whole look screamed "Old Maid," and I wasn't fooled by the "Mrs." moniker. People called my Aunt Agnes "Mrs." and she wasn't married to anybody unless you counted her poodle.

The first time Mrs. Stull arrived she sat down on the piano bench, patting the space next to her to indicate where I was to sit. The problem is, she took up two and a half feet of the three foot bench, so I could only park one of my butt cheeks on the space allotted while the other cheek hung over the edge.

Every lesson began the same way — she would play a little ditty comprised of about 10 notes and then look at me with a hopeful expression, as if trying to communicate with a chimpanzee. She didn't say anything, she just played and looked, played and looked. When I just sat there staring at her, she must have realized I didn't have the talent (or intelligence?) of a chimpanzee, but instead of saying, "Now, why don't you try it?" or something to indicate what she wanted me to do, she simply played the same passage again, only louder. Then she played it again. And again. And again. Each time she would pound the last note with finality, as if pounding a nail. And each time she would look at me, expectantly. She seemed determined not to speak to me and frankly, I didn't know what she wanted me to do. Did she want me to commandeer the piano and shove her off the bench? Did she want me to sing? Jump up and dance? Go get a cookie and wander off to play? (No. I tried that, and it turns out that wasn't what she wanted.)

Get this: she honestly expected me to do exactly what she had just done! This became abundantly clear when she grabbed my stubby little fingers, molded them into a claw-shaped fist and then reached in and extracted my thumb. "This goes right here," she said, plunking it down on middle C. "This is called C and it is where we always start." Then, peeling my index finger out of its balled-up state, she pounded it onto the D key. "And this is D."

At this point I couldn't get past her first statement, "C is where we always start." *You might want to mention that to my first-grade teacher, Mrs. Stull. She's under the impression we always start with "A" then "B" and THEN "C."*

But while I was having this little conversation in my head she had already started to unravel my middle finger and press it onto the E key. "And this is E," she announced triumphantly, as if I couldn't figure out that E came after D.

It would be years before I would select my E finger as my favorite and most often used. If only I'd known its meaning then!

After she had identified each of the keys we returned to C — since that's where we always start — and she took my thumb again and banged it on the key. "Play!" she commanded, and I tentatively struck the key. "Again!" she said. "Again!" "Again!"

I don't know if you've ever sat at a piano and struck the same key repeatedly, but let's just say it gets old fast — and you can't hum it later.

I was so relieved when, some six hours later (or maybe 20 minutes in real time) she said, "Well, that's enough."

She slipped out of the house without saying anything to my grandmother and I honestly hoped that would be the last time we saw her. When my grandmother asked how the lesson had gone, I said, "She said she was never coming back."

"I doubt that," my grandmother replied knowingly. And she was right. Mrs. Stull returned like toe fungus every week for the next year or so, until I finally got it through to my grandmother that I would do something drastic if she kept forcing me to play that stupid piano.

But the truth is, I've always wished she hadn't caved in. That's why some sixty years later and as part of my recent campaign to slow our mental decline, I insisted we buy a piano.

"It will be good for us," I told Brad. "It will force us to use our minds…to discover something new…."

And we did! We discovered we can't play the piano and don't want to learn!

But at least it looks good in the living room — and it's always there when people drop in and want to play a tune, which we encourage them to do. Just don't play the same note over and over. That lid can be slammed, you know. Hard.

It's Only a Suggestion, Not a Rule

We have a nice little group of friends in the gated community where we live.

("Gated community?" Brad says. "Prisons are 'gated communities,' you know!" So allow me to state for the record: we don't live in a prison.)

But it is a tight-knit little neighborhood and we enjoy getting together frequently for dinners, cook-outs or just cocktails.

So, when our across-the-street neighbors Doug and Brenda recently invited us to come see them, we readily accepted. We envisioned a trip of maybe 100 feet or so, most likely with a bottle of Champagne in our hands.

But it turns out they were inviting us to their other home — in Edmonton, Alberta. *Canada*.

"Canada!" we gasped. "Won't we freeze to death?"

Doug and Brenda assured us that summer was quite tolerable in Edmonton (but note they didn't mention winter — and why would they? That's when they're down here in California!)

So, we thought, "Why not?"

Living in a resort community, one learns very quickly

that things are different "off-season." For example, we can find non-stop flights to lots of cities — from Seattle to New York — during the "season," but off-season... well, how does a Greyhound Bus sound?

Not really. We were able to fly on WestJet, a little airline we'd never heard of but turned out to be quite pleasant.

Days later, as we were preparing to return home via Vancouver, we approached the ticket counter to check in for our flight and were directed to an automated kiosk. But since a uniformed agent was standing idle nearby, I decided I would forego the learning curve on the machine and ask him to help us in person.

"Excuse me," I said. "Must I use this kiosk?"

"Well," he said, "Well, nobody's holding a gun to your head."

I like a snarky, sarcastic answer like that, so I smiled and piled our bags on his scale. Maybe doing some work would improve his demeanor.

Laughing about that exchange as we walked to the gate, we realized that was pretty much the attitude wherever we went in Canada. There are rules, yes, and everybody agrees that things go more smoothly if you follow them. But if you don't? Well, nobody will hold a gun to your head.

Doug and Brenda have a lovely home across the street from us in Palm Springs, but their home in Canada is even nicer. (And big!) They have a gorgeous lawn and garden in the back, bordering on a large forested area. An eight-foot privacy fence provides a nice backdrop to the explosion of blooms and greenery everywhere you look.

We were sitting out there our first evening when Doug

nonchalantly said, "Oh, we should forewarn you — you might hear some coyotes tonight."

That put me on high alert, of course, since it is well-known that I'm not a big fan of nature.

"What do you mean, 'coyotes'?" I asked. "And what do you mean, 'hear'? What exactly will they be saying?"

"Oh, they howl," Brenda said casually. "And when they hear sirens in the neighborhood, that sets them off too."

As if on cue, we heard a siren and I braced myself for the howling. Sure enough, we heard one...then two... then three...then ten *thousand* coyotes — just on the other side of the fence! I swear I saw the gate moving while the howling was going on.

It appears that Doug and Brenda have purchased a home next door to a wild animal preserve or a coyote breeding ground or...who knows what. I began squirming in my seat and nervously kept an eye on the sliding patio door to make sure I could reach it in time if the gate came crashing down and we were suddenly attacked by a mob (herd? coven?) of coyotes.

The siren finally stopped and the howling eventually died down, but I was rattled. Later, when we went to bed, Brad insisted on leaving the window partially open for "air," since he suffers from the belief that all rooms are hermetically sealed. I studied the window, trying to determine whether a coyote could fit through it.

We were just about asleep when out of the dark night sky there arose such a chorus of howling that I tried to remember if we'd left Doug and Brenda outdoors — fearing, I suppose, that they were being torn to shreds by a pack of wolves. (Coyotes, as everybody knows, turn into wolves at night. Look it up.)

I looked at Brad and he looked at me — I swear his pupils were glowing red — and all I can say is that if he had run one of those toenails down my leg at that point, they would have had to scrape me off the ceiling.

The next day I unobtrusively checked for blood stains on the deck and outdoor furniture, and finding none I decided maybe it would be okay to stay another night after all.

We're all different (but some are more different than others, as some wag pointed out) and that certainly applies to the differences between Americans and Canadians. I discovered, for example, that Canadians don't rinse their dishes before putting them in the dishwasher.

I think this is a brilliant idea — one I thought of myself — but Brad never bought into it and will actually take a dish out of the dishwasher that I have put in, simply to "rinse" it. He is adamant that dishes must be thoroughly rinsed before they are placed in the dishwasher. This is something I refuse to do, so after a year or so of my loading dirty dishes and him taking them out to rinse, he finally said, "I'll tell you what. You don't need to handle the dirty dishes at all. I'll do it."

So that worked out fine, didn't it?

Imagine my glee when I discovered quite by accident that Brenda's dishwasher was full of dishes that obviously hadn't been rinsed! I could hardly wait to tell Brad.

"Guess what!" I said. "Brenda doesn't rinse her dishes before placing them in the dishwasher!" I refrained from adding, "So there!"

Without missing a beat he said, "No wonder they have coyotes hanging around."

* * *

"To welcome you to Canada," Brenda said on the day of our arrival, "we have arranged to have our windows washed."

I smiled politely, thinking what a cute way to admit that you would be conducting your regular cleaning routines regardless of whether or not you had guests present. But when the window washer showed up I realized they really did it as a treat for us.

The name of the window washing company was "Men in Kilts."

Sure enough, that's what the hunky guy was wearing when he came to the door: an authentic kilt, with a squeegee hanging on the side where his sword might have been.

To complete the ensemble, he wore a T-shirt inscribed with the words, "No Peeking."

That didn't sit well with me. Strictly from a professional standpoint, having spent the better part of my life in public relations and marketing, I knew that such a negative message would never result in repeat business.

So I decided to tell him as much.

We all sat on the deck as he worked — I admit that I was watching him very closely, from, um, a marketing perspective — when I finally got up enough nerve to tell him what a stupid slogan "No Peeking" was.

He listened politely as I talked about its negative message, and how in the context of repeat business, it would never work, blah, blah, blah. I had the feeling he might have heard this thinly-veiled come-on before and was just patronizing me, nodding his head up and down as I spoke. (As it turns out, that's a Canadian thing and can't be helped.)

When I finished, he smiled and said, "Well, it's just a suggestion, not a rule."

Okay, then!

That's not to say they don't have rules in Canada. A few days later we were in Vancouver, in Stanley Park, about to have lunch. Brad decided on a burger and after verbalizing his choice to the server, he added, "Medium-well, please."

She cocked her head slightly as if she hadn't quite heard him correctly and then, in a voice normally reserved for addressing five year-olds, she said, "Oh, I'm sorry. In Canada, burgers are always well done." And with that she turned on her heels and headed for the kitchen!

But she's right, of course. Everything in Canada is well done, indeed!

Couldn't You Just Die?

While eating out recently, I was eavesdropping on two women talking loudly at the table next to me as I waited for Brad to come back from the men's room.

"Did you hear that thing about Jane and the toilet paper?" an attractive looking blond woman asked her lunch partner, who was also attractive and blond and the only reason I know this is because when I turned around to see who was speaking I scanned the room and noticed that every woman in the room was blond. What was this, a Loreal convention?

So the second blond (yes, I'm now reduced to numbering them) says to the first, "Oh, yes! Can you imagine? Walking down the aisle of her daughter's wedding with toilet paper stuck to her shoe!? I would have *died!*"

Blond #1 laughingly replied, "Yes, me too! *Died!*"

Brad wandered back to the table during all this talk about death and toilet paper. After I gave him a friendly greeting consisting of holding my index finger in front of my lips and hissing "Shhh," I continued to listen while staring at him as if I were in a trance. He stared back at me as if I were crazy.

But by this time Blond #1 had introduced a new topic, something to do with her son's school and I lost interest, so I returned my attention to Brad.

"Did you hear that," I whispered — knowing full well that he didn't because he was in the Men's Room at the time and he probably wouldn't have heard it anyway even if he'd been sitting on their laps and they had been addressing each other with megaphones.

"That woman said she would have died! Over toilet paper stuck to her shoe!"

As you might expect, my thoughtful and pragmatic Brad had just one question: "Why didn't someone stop and tell her — or better yet, remove it for her?"

Why, indeed? Especially since she almost *died*.

That reminded me of another toilet paper incident which, I suspect, was intended to cause *me* to die of embarrassment, but didn't.

Years earlier, in a different restaurant in a different city, my friend David left the table for five minutes and came back dragging an entire *roll* of toilet paper behind him all the way across the restaurant. He did it to be funny and to try to embarrass me. But by that point in our friendship I was immune to his pranks as he had, among other things, once picked me up at my office driving an antique fire truck with the siren blaring and the bell clanging. So leaving a trail of toilet paper across the floor of an expensive restaurant was nothing.

When I told this story to the ever-curious Brad, he said, "How did he get the toilet paper to unroll without causing it to break at one of the perforations?"

He said that. Perforations. This is what I put up with.

I explained that David had unrolled the entire roll and carried the loose pile just outside the door of the restroom and dropped it before he began walking toward the table.

"How was it stuck to his shoe?"

"I don't know — he probably tucked it into the back of his shoe…oh, never mind!"

The word that stood out to me in the Conversation of the Blondes was the repeated use of the word *die*. Both women said they could have "died" due, presumably, to the embarrassment of having toilet paper on your shoe.

Let's agree that they may be guilty of hyperbole. I know, because I almost used it once myself.

But there are many things that might cause us to "almost die," not the least of which are serious car accidents (been there, done that — twice); falling off a ladder (I did that while putting the outdoor Christmas decorations on my parents' house); drowning (at 10 years old I was rescued by a woman wearing a dress while the life guard chatted with a pretty girl); and, of course, choking on a piece of food.

Most people don't know this, but between 8,000-10,000 people die each year in the United States from choking on food.

I know, because I was almost one of them. Three times.

Before you make nasty judgments about me not chewing my food properly, that applies to only one of the three incidents, the one with the bacon.

Now I should quickly mention that it wasn't the bacon's fault. I love bacon. Brad and I each eat exactly 730 pieces of bacon *each* per year. How do I know this?

Because we have two pieces of bacon every single day at breakfast (along with two eggs and an English muffin) and there are *no exceptions.*

On this particular occasion, however — the one during which I almost choked to death — I hadn't yet met Brad and the bacon I was eating was part of a B.L.T. sandwich.

I've often wondered in the years since if I was actually *trying* to choke myself to death so I could stop listening to the woman who had invited me to lunch. She had been talking non-stop from the time we sat down, complaining about her husband, who was one of my best friends. I didn't like what she was saying and I knew it wasn't true, but I hadn't been able to get a word in edgewise as she continued to ramble on. That must have been when I sub-consciously decided to choke to death.

At first I was just startled. I knew something was lodged in my throat, but it never occurred to me that it wouldn't un-lodge itself and continue on its merry way.

I tried to clear my throat.

I tried to clear it again.

I tried a third time, even as I felt panic rising.

Meanwhile, my lunch partner never stopped talking. I looked at her with my eyes open as wide as they get and grabbed my throat.

She didn't even inhale. The words continued to pour out as I began to wonder if she would still be talking when I fell out of my chair onto the floor. I didn't want to be rude, but I finally decided I would have to take matters into my own hands. I got up from the table, turned on my heels and headed straight to the kitchen. As far as I knew, she was still talking.

In the kitchen, things happened quickly. I was

probably white as a ghost and was certainly covered with sweat, so when I stumbled through the swinging door a waiter intercepted me and said, "Are you choking?"

I nodded and without another word, he whirled me around, placed his hands around my waist and pulled me into him as hard as he could.

It worked! The famous Heimlich Maneuver actually works! The bacon flew across the room landing who knows where as I gasped a lung full of air, glorious air.

To the waiter I said, "Thank you thank you thank you thank you…" and he smiled shyly and said, "No problem, sir. It happens all the time."

"It *does*?" I wanted to say. What a job! I fished out my wallet and gave him all the cash I had — about a hundred dollars. I wadded it all up and thrust it into his hand as I tried to shake his hand off in gratitude. It's funny how we take air for granted until we don't have it for a few minutes. "Thank you thank you thank you…," I kept repeating.

Returning to the table I found my dining partner still seated with a blank look on her face.

"Was something wrong?" she asked dryly.

I wanted to shout, "Yes! I almost choked to death!" But instead I just said, "Yes, but it's okay now."

Fortunately, before she could get her second wind, the manager came over and said, "Sir, I hope you're okay."

Embarrassed, I said, "Yes, yes, everything is fine. Thank you and your staff for the way you took care of me."

"Yes, but…," he said. "Of course we called 9-1-1…."

"Oh my," I said, relieved that I wouldn't be leaving in a body bag. "I assume you called them back to tell them all is well…?"

"Um...yes...but unfortunately they were already on their way and they are required to verify first hand that you are no longer in danger, so I expect they'll be arriving shortly...."

With that I said to Ms. Chatterbox, "Well, that's my cue. I don't want to create more of a scene than I already have. (This seemed to puzzle her, but I forged ahead.) Thank you for an interesting lunch, but I really do think you need to tell your husband everything you've told me."

Sure enough, on the way through the parking lot to my car I heard the sirens approaching and within seconds a big hook and ladder truck roared into the parking lot. (What, did they think I was on the roof? With an ambulance right behind?)

People stopped and stared, but I kept walking, right past half a dozen of the most gorgeous firemen I'd ever seen, one of whom gave me a big brilliant smile.

I could have *died*!

What I Almost Had in Common with Bette Davis

When you read this chapter you may wonder if this whole book is going to be about my choking incidents.

No. This is the last time I'll mention it, so stop complaining. After all, I was the one choking, not you.

My second choking incident was at a business luncheon a few months after my "bacon blunder," and it caused me to ask my doctor if there was something wrong with my throat since I seemed to be choking with some frequency.

The culprit this time wasn't a piece of bacon but, rather a piece of filet mignon. (I know: what a diet, right?) In my defense, the meals were ordered in advance and we were all having the same thing: steak salad.

I was a minor player at this luncheon, so everybody's attention was directed to the big shot at the other end of the table when I realized I had a bite of steak lodged in my throat. This time I didn't wait until I almost passed out; I simply got up, placed my napkin neatly on my chair (to indicate that I would be returning, which is the proper thing to do) and walked into the kitchen.

In those few steps the chunk of meat had completely shut off my air supply, and the moment I walked through the swinging door I knew I was about to keel over. Once again, a waiter intercepted me and asked if I was choking. (Where do they find these people?!) I nodded, he twirled me around, and pulled me with such force that he lifted me off the ground. (Fun!) The steak flew out, I paid him his hundred dollars and returned to the table, with no one the wiser.

Oh. When I gave him the money — with my eternal thanks — I said, "I'm begging you — do NOT call 9-1-1. I'm fine — really." Thankfully, he didn't, although I'd love to have seen the look on that fireman's face this time!

The third — and shall we hope, final — incident took place a few years ago in Paris, at a nondescript little cafe atop Montmartre, just around the corner from the Sacré-Coeur.

We were a party of six, having been joined by two of our California neighbors and two of their friends who were touring Paris together.

It should be noted that exactly twelve houses separate us from these friends at home, but Paris is where we had dinner with them.

We were seated outdoors in a typical (touristy) French cafe. It was a lovely early evening, and the views of Paris were spectacular from up there. We had just been served what Americans call our entrees but which the wacky French insist on calling the "plat" (main course). (The entrée is, of course, the appetizer.)

My *plat* was seafood (no bacon or steak for me,

thanks!) — a trout-like fish called a Dorade. When it arrived, I specifically asked if it had been de-boned (fileted) in the kitchen. *"Est ce poisson sans os?"*

"Oui, Monsieur," he said, lying through his teeth — because, as I was about to discover, the fish was nothing *but* bones, and it took about ten seconds for one of them to become lodged sideways in my throat.

This time I could still breathe, thankfully, and also drink (excellent!). So I began by alternating sips of air with sips of wine, then water, then air, then forced coughing which quickly became tiresome for the other diners, so I excused myself and walked over to a wall at the edge of the mountain and tried to throw up.

In retrospect this must have been quite a scene from the table. While my friends are trying to enjoy their meals, I'm across the street, doubled over, making throwing-up noises and literally trying to gag myself so I'll vomit the bone out.

But it wasn't budging. Brad came across the street and pounded me on the back a few dozen times before asking if he could have the glass of wine that had just been poured for me.

"Yes," I hissed, "but we'll need a taxi *tout de suite!*"

"Why?" he asked, genuinely concerned.

"Because I need to go to the hospital to get this stupid bone out of my throat."

Long story short (or still long, I guess), a taxi was called, we told our friends we would see them back in the 'hood,' and off we went, headed for the American Hospital of Paris, a few *arrondissements* away.

On the way, in the taxi, I pulled out my phone and typed into Google Translate, "I am choking. I have a bone stuck in my throat. Please help."

I pushed Translate and the message appeared on my screen: *"Je m'étouffe. J'ai un os coincé dans la gorge. S'il vous plaît aider."* By this time the pain was excruciating and tears welled up in my eyes.

Well, if I walk in crying they'll surely realize it's important, I thought.

I tapped the phone screen periodically so the message wouldn't go away.

Curiously, the woman at the reception desk at the American Hospital of Paris does not speak English, so I was glad I had my phone to push into her face.

"Oui!" she said, picking up the phone and dialing a number.

"Who's she calling?" I asked Brad.

"The doctor, I hope," he said.

After hanging up, she told us to go down a long hall, turn right, take the elevator to the third floor, turn left, follow another long hall and go into a room and wait for the doctor.

"Huh?" I said.

"I'll show you," said Brad. "Follow me."

"Have you been here before?" I whispered through my fishbone. "How do you know where to go?"

"Just follow me," he said. So I did.

Later, we would remember that the hospital corridors were almost dark — we turned on lights as we went — and we never saw another patient. The entire experience would make a great horror movie.

Not long after we sat down in the room we had been told to sit in, the door burst open and some teenager, dressed head-to-toe in black leather and carrying a motorcycle helmet, marched past us into the adjoining room.

"Ha!" I said, "With my luck that'll be the doctor."

As if on cue, the motorcyclist reappeared and asked if I had a fishbone caught in my throat.

"Yes," I managed to mumble, wondering what business it was of his.

"I'm doctor so-and-so," he said in perfect English. "Follow me."

I looked at Brad with horror but we both fell in line and followed the leather-clad "doctor" to an examination room. His helmet was placed on a desk nearby.

He gestured to where I should sit and rolled up a stool beside me. "Open wide, please."

I did this before I noticed that he hadn't washed his hands and wasn't wearing rubber gloves. But before I could say anything, he thrust his thumb and forefinger down my throat, and it was all I could do to keep from biting them off.

He withdrew his hand and said, "It's really down there, isn't it?"

I was too dumbfounded to speak.

At this point he conjured up a pair of forceps and it didn't take much imagination to guess where they'd be going — or where they'd been. As far as I could tell, they hadn't been wrapped in paper or plastic and didn't come out of a sterilization oven or jar of herbicide of any sort (even my barber has one of those, for combs!). But I just wanted to get this over with and figured I could always get a tetanus shot later, so I opened wide.

But my tongue had other plans.

The two of them — my tongue and the dirty steel forceps — immediately began dueling for access to my throat.

I saw the doctor recoil at what was obviously a demon-possessed snake tongue. Mick Jagger had taken over my throat!

The tongue needed to be subdued. Taking a piece of surgical gauze (sterile or not — who knows), he grabbed my tongue with the gauze and his forceps with the other.

Unbeknownst to me, Brad had in the meantime sneaked up behind me and said to the doctor, "May I help?"

Well, this almost put me over the edge. I spit out the doctor's gauze-wrapped fingers and said, "Help? Help do what!? You are a Ph.D. for heaven's sake. You didn't go to medical school! If the doctor needs help with a German Literature question, we'll summon you. Meanwhile, please go sit down."

This made the doctor smile. I laughed at my own hilarious delivery, and as I did he grabbed my tongue again with his piece of gauze.

Then, as if by magic, he plunged the pincers down my throat and pulled out — a bone!

I told people later I thought it was my ankle bone, but it really wasn't that big — but it wasn't small either. Finally, I could swallow again. I was healed!

And with that, Moto-Doc, as I now refer to him, said "That will be 200 euros, please," which we paid in cash and which he slipped into the pocket of his tight leather pants. Then, after putting the helmet back on his head, he walked out ahead of us, letting us find our own way.

When we were safely outdoors I said to Brad, "Between the lack of sterilized equipment and the doctor's bare fingers down my throat, let's just say I am unimpressed with the American Hospital of Paris."

Or, as Bette Davis might say — who, in 1989, died in

this same hospital, "What a dump!"

Historical footnote: *The American Hospital of Paris was founded in 1906. It remains private/non-profit and is not part of the French national healthcare system. Other famous patients — who hopefully had a better experience than Bette Davis — include Rock Hudson, Gertrude Stein, and Aristotle Onassis. There is no word on whether their doctors wore black leather outfits or washed their hands.*

Crazy Lady at the Movies

If I have any vices (and oh, baby, do I!) one of them has got to be how much I love going to the movies. This has been true my entire life, beginning with "Bambi," which I saw in 1954 or 1955 when I was six or seven years old.

"Bambi" was a curious choice given the circumstances of my life at the time.

The movie, as you may recall, is a Disney animated film about a baby deer. It was made in 1942 for $858,000. That is a pittance compared to the cost of making a movie today. The latest Spiderman movie, for example, cost $268 *million.*

But old Uncle Walt did okay on his little animated fawn — that measly $858,000 investment has earned him and estate over $267 *million* to-date.

The story, in case you've forgotten, is about the little deer who is destined to one day take over the role of Great Prince of the Forest from his father. Bambi makes various friends along the way, including a rabbit named Thumper and a skunk named Flower.

Sounds pretty safe for a six-year old to see, right?

Not so fast, Bub. The movie quickly takes a dark turn

when "Man" is introduced (ain't that always the case!) and Bambi's mother, to whom he is completely devoted, is shot dead.

That's right: d-e-a-d. The beautiful mama deer took a bullet before I'd finished half my popcorn.

Oh well. Stuff happens, right? That's part of life, right?

Yes, but the six-year old in question — me — had just lost his own mother the year before. By the end of the movie somehow my own mom's death became conflated with Bambi's mom's death in my tiny brain, and I am told I was inconsolable for weeks afterward.

But in an effort to comfort me, I suppose, my caretakers (grandmother and aunt) got me a dog, "Buffer" — a dog of indeterminate heritage with short blond fur, and big sad eyes. Buffer and I bonded immediately.

Then, in what I assume is complete happenstance, they took me to see a movie about a dog: "Old Yeller." You remember "Old Yeller," don't you? A sweet dog with short blond fur and big sad eyes — like my very own Buffer! But this is a movie in which the title star must be shot — killed — by its boy-owner. In other words, not a comedy.

I'm told I was so bereft at the end of the movie they had to wait until the theater lights came on and all the patrons had gone before they could get me out of there.

Frankly, I'm surprised anybody was ever able to get me to go to another movie after those two tear-jerkers, but somehow they did and eventually I learned that all those emotions — sadness, laughter, fear, etc. — can be cathartic. In time, I fell in love with motion pictures and am in love with the experience of going to the movies to this day.

And no, not just because of the popcorn.

Not long ago we went to see an "art film." That's usually code for "movies with sub-titles," but not in this particular case. The movie was "Rebel in the Rye," a story about the life of author J.D. Salinger. Most people have read or heard of Salinger's best-selling book, "Catcher in the Rye."

Before I go on, I should mention that I have all kinds of "rules" when going to the movies:

- I must sit on the end of a row because I feel claustrophobic if others are blocking me in;

- We must arrive early enough to see all of the previews;

- There is to be absolutely no talking;

- And one of the most important of all: we sit through the credits at the end. All of them. Don't you want to know who scouted the locations and did the casting? How can you leave the theater without knowing who the "Best Boy" was? (Or what a "Best Boy" is, for that matter.)

The real reason I make us wait until all the credits have been shown is that I have a son who has his Master's degree from film school and his name will someday be up on that screen. When that happens, I can promise you that if people know what's good for them, *nobody* will leave that theater before the credits end!

One of the nice things about staying till the bitter end is the fact that sometimes you are rewarded with the outtakes and bloopers that occurred during the making of the film. Some of the funniest scenes I have ever seen in a movie came at the end of Melissa McCarthy's "This is Forty." And we were the only people to see them! (Serves you right, you rude people who insist on tripping down the stairs — and over my feet — while the theater is still dark.)

So back to "Rebel in the Rye." After the credits ended, a young woman who had been sitting on the opposite side of the theater in the row in front of us suddenly appeared to my left, scaring me half to death. I had already turned to see that the theater was empty so Brad and I could begin our critique of the movie (talking during the credits is allowed), so where did this person come from?

The first words out of her mouth were, in a loud voice, "Have you read the book?" Clearly, she was agitated about something.

I confess that I scanned her to see if she was carrying a gun or a knife because she was acting a little crazy.

(When I say I "scanned her," I mean I looked her over. I didn't run her through an x-ray machine.)

"You mean 'Catcher in the Rye'?" I asked.

"Yes," she snapped. "Did you ever read it?"

"Um, yes. In high school," I replied.

"Well, I didn't," she reported, at which point I assumed this bizarre conversation would end. But no....

"I've had a terrible day," she said.

I was getting ready to ask what was wrong with her — in every sense of the word — but she continued, unprompted.

"My husband died last month."

"Oh no," I said, remembering that grief makes many people crazy. "I'm so sorry." And I meant it.

"No, that's okay," she said — those were her exact words — "but what really has me upset is that the new

Apple iPhone came out today…."

I must have looked confused. True, I don't like some of the features on the new iPhone either, but I'm not sure that would overshadow, say, the death of a loved one.

Noticing my bewilderment, she continued, "Actually, I took it in for repair yesterday and I was supposed to pick it up today."

I continued staring at her, eyebrows knit.

Now she sounded a bit impatient, like I'm a dunce for not understanding the depth of the tragedy she was describing. "And, you know…new phone….long lines around the block to get in the Apple Store…."

At that point I actually did begin to understand — sort of. I would never go near an Apple Store on the day of a new product launch.

But I still didn't know how to respond. I'd already said I was so sorry, but that was about her dead husband — not the inconvenience of having to wait in a long line to pick up a cell phone. I decided we all have our own ways of grieving, so who was I to judge her behavior?

At this point she sat down in the seat next to me and began to ramble about this and that: Apple products… living in a resort down…annoying people…other movies…etc. Brad and I sat and listened for a while and somehow she started to pull herself together. The more she talked, the calmer she became.

As we herded her up the aisle and out of the theater I thought of a quote from "Catcher in the Rye" which was referenced in the movie we'd just seen. "…I'm standing on the edge of some crazy cliff. What I have to do, I have to catch everybody if they start to go over the cliff — I mean if they're running and they don't look where they're going I have to come out from somewhere and *catch* them. That's all I'd do all day. I'd just be the catcher in the rye and all."

I guess we all need to be more aware of people who are about to go off the cliff. Maybe there's an iPhone app for that.

Original of Mind

I've never been big on horoscopes — unless I happen to read one I agree with, then I'm a big believer.

On my birthday in 1980, somebody named "Stella" — whom I've never met — wrote in her newspaper column that I was "Original of mind and strong of body." I'm not sure what "original of mind" means, unless it is another way of saying, "You're one of a kind," which could apply to Lizzie Borden as easily as Madame Curie, so I'm not sure that's such a compliment.

But I do know what "strong of body" is, and I'm positive it doesn't describe me. At the gym I can leg press 200 pounds without too much effort, yet I can't stand on one leg for longer than twenty seconds without tipping over. And while I don't have any trouble adjusting the TV on the treadmill, it's all I can do to stay on it once the belt starts moving. And when Trevor the Trainer handed me two straps attached to the ends of a big rubber band and then ordered me to "squat as though you plan to sit," that's just what I did: I sat, and stayed.

So, no, I don't think "strong of body" applies to me.

A year later, Stella had more to say. That year she decided I had "a difficult time either asking for or accepting advice from others," but I was "quick to offer it."

Hey, wait a minute. In other words, I can dish it out but I can't take it — is that what you're saying, STELLA?

Who asked her!?

That same year she went on to say that I "enjoy things that are bigger than life: huge enterprises, flamboyant people, extravagant emotions, exceptional risk, etc.," and I must admit there is some truth to that. I love the idea of going to the moon — that's certainly a huge enterprise — but I don't like swimming in the ocean, so I'm not sure I qualify as liking "exceptional risk."

"Extravagant emotions" is a definite yes — I've been known to cry during movie *previews* and once laughed so loud and long that my friend and I were asked to leave a lecture hall.

So the jury may be out on the subject of horoscopes, but fortune cookies are a different matter. How could anybody doubt the wisdom of a fortune cookie?

Like any sensible person, I refuse to eat a fortune cookie if it contains a fortune I dislike or disagree with, but if I like it, I'll save it, tucking the best ones into my wallet for "later." Two of these have been there for at least twenty years, hiding out in the same compartment as my driver's license — which will make them easy to find if I get pulled over by a police officer.

"Yes, here's my driver's license, officer — and...well what do you know, here's a cookie fortune for you! Let's see what it says. Why, I'll be darned. It says 'Your kindness will lead you to happiness.' Hmmmm. I wonder what that means!"

If this doesn't work — that is, if he doesn't live up to the fortune cookie's instruction, I will say, "Oops, my mistake. That one's mine. Here's yours..." and then I'll pull out an actual fortune I received in a cookie at least thirty years ago. It is one-sided — nothing written on the back — and on the front is written only one word: "Fish."

That ought to do it.

For fun, I looked up "Best fortune cookie quotes," and they don't get much better than these:

"We don't know the future, but here's a cookie."

"Help! I am being held prisoner in a fortune cookie factory!"

"That wasn't chicken."

"All fortunes are wrong except this one."

"When you squeeze an orange, orange juice comes out — because that's what's inside."

"You are sensitive, kind, thoughtful, wise, generous and gullible."

Yes, that's me — gullible. And that applies to everybody else who takes horoscopes and fortune cookies seriously.

Unless they're being offered by a certified fortune

teller, of course.

Years ago, my friends Liz and Gerry picked me up in a limousine so we could go to lunch to celebrate our birthdays, which are within a few days of each other. Large quantities of champagne were called for, so Liz and Gerry thoughtfully arranged for a car and driver.

On the way home from the restaurant, Liz spotted a "Fortune Teller" sign on the street we were driving down and said to the driver, "Pull in here, please."

"Let's have our fortunes told!" she said.

"What a good idea!" Gerry replied.

"I'll drink to that!" I said, and did.

The fortune teller's "cottage," if you want to call it that, was just big enough for the three of us to squeeze into, with a tiny room in the back where the fortune teller herself hung out. The whole place was darkish but with a string of white Christmas lights and about a dozen candles perched on the table and shelves. It was light enough for me to see that we were about to be duped.

The fortune teller was an attractive, middle-aged woman with a serious look. She was wearing what appeared to be a kaftan or muumuu, and she had rings on every finger including her thumbs.

I had to bite my tongue to keep from saying, "Less is more, dear."

Liz got to go first — I forget why — and she was in the backroom for about 30 minutes. She was the same old Liz when she came out — I guess I was afraid the fortune teller would steal her 3-carat diamond ring, but she was still wearing it when she reappeared, smiling broadly and saying, "You won't believe this...."

"Don't tell us yet!" we said in unison. We wanted to be surprised. But after Gerry went in, Liz told me everything she'd just been told.

I don't remember now exactly what it was, but it was all positive and sounded sincere and, according to Liz and from everything I knew about her, *spot on.*

Gerry went next and from her look when she returned, we could see that the fortune teller had done it again.

Now it was my turn and you have never seen anyone more skeptical in your life.

The fortune teller — let's call her Betty — began by taking both my hands and holding them in hers. She gazed deep into my eyes at which time I noticed that one of her eyebrows was wonky — it had been drawn on crooked. I briefly wondered if I should tell her.

You seem surprised, I thought about saying. *Or at least half-surprised, since that one eyebrow seems to have a mind of its own....*

But I didn't say a thing. I just looked into her eyes — one of which was lazy, so I decided that perhaps she'd drawn that one eyebrow on in such a way as to compensate for her lazy eye. Sort of as if she were saying, "Don't look at my lazy eye — look at my wonky eyebrow!"

I was baffled.

But she promptly brought me back to reality — or what passed for reality after a couple of bottles of champagne — when she said, "You're going through a divorce, aren't you?"

That sobered me up pretty quickly, because it was true. I quickly checked to see if my wedding ring was still in place — I had made a conscious decision to keep wearing it until the divorce was final — and it was right there on my left hand.

"Yes," I mumbled. "I guess Liz told you."

"No," she said emphatically. "Your friends didn't tell me anything." I believed her.

Next she said, "Your soon to be ex-wife is moving to Omaha."

I'm sure this caused the color to drain out of my face because my kids had just told me the week before that their mother was in Nebraska for the weekend. When I asked why Nebraska, they told me because the single man across the street had a second house there.

But move? Never. I was about to tell her as much when her eyebrow told me to shut up.

"You have two children, don't you?"

I nodded.

"They will be fine — and so will you. You will quit your job and move to be with them."

Yeah, right. I had lived in Denver all my life and I knew I wasn't going anywhere — certainly not Omaha. And neither were my kids if I had anything to do with it. Not only that, I loved my job and would never leave it.

I don't remember what else was said, but I know we opened our fourth bottle of champagne the minute we got back in the car. The driver ended up having to walk us up to our front doors when he dropped each of us off.

At least I learned something valuable from that experience: fortune tellers don't know squat. It's a scam. It's meaningless. It's all a joke, and here's how I know: my wife didn't move to Omaha. She moved to Houston.

And it was a whole month before I quit my job and left Denver for good.

But she was right about one thing: my kids were fine — and so was I.

Signs

And the sign said, 'long-haired freaky people need not apply…"
Signs, signs, everywhere a sign….do this, don't do that, can't you read the sign?

- Les Emmerson

The authorities recently put up a red stop sign in our neighborhood that says "STOP — AT ALL TIMES."

Huh? Does that mean I can choose whether or not I stop at the other stop signs? We have approximately twenty stop signs in our neighborhood and until now I thought they all meant that I had to stop "at all times."

But now I'm wondering if I've been wasting my time.

The truth is, people in the U.S. love signs. In France and several other European countries I can think of, you don't see "sign clutter" the way you do here.

Not that they don't have a few here and there, but usually they aren't in English, so it's fun to try to figure out what you shouldn't be doing right before you do it.

For example, one day I was hiking just outside a small village in Austria when I came upon a sign that said

"Wanderweges ist verboten!" If a sign is in German, it's usually best to do as it says, which in this case was not to wanderwege. I ignored it and wanderwegged my way down the trail until I came to a fork in the road and a sign with only one word printed on it: "Wiesenrunde." That was the name of the village where I wanted to go, so I stopped to study the sign carefully.

As previously stated, there was only one word — the name of the village — but below it there were two arrows, one pointing to the left (down the wanderwegging trail) and the other to the right (down the other wanderwegging trail.) I wasn't sure what to do. The arrows were professionally printed on the sign, not just scribbled on it by some Austrian mountain goat, so I had to make a decision: left or right? At first I chose left, but then I decided that wasn't right.

At some point I came across a large sign at the edge of the trail that said, "Mooshott."

I found a big rock nearby and sat on it so I could study the sign to figure out what it meant. There weren't any arrows, so I knew it wasn't directing me anywhere. I looked at the GPS on my phone but there wasn't any mention of a town or village named "Mooshott," so finally I gave up and started walking again.

The trail soon turned into a road and I had to stop and turn around to make sure I hadn't taken a wrong fork. No, the dirt and rock trail I had been walking on had simply become a paved road, as though at some time in history somebody walking down that same trail said to themselves, "I'll bet someday they will invent a contraption that runs on gasoline and has four rubber tires and can be controlled by people who don't know how to use their turn signals, so let's pave this trail from here on!"

That may or may not have been what really happened, but it was certainly true that a moment earlier I was walking on a mountain trail and now I was walking down the middle of a paved roadway.

I also noted that there were now fences on both sides of the road, and since I hadn't come through a gate of any kind, I realized that if I were driving in the opposite direction on this road I would eventually be driving on a dirt path into a field of grass and flowers and — in the middle of this profound thought — I stopped short to keep from stepping in a pile of poop, deposited by one of Austria's national pets, a cow.

Ah ha! I think I just figured out what Moo Shott is! And thank heaven I didn't step in it.

The next sign I came to was "Rettenegg," but that was in the style of sign they use to announce that you are entering a city or town in Austria, so I knew I was approaching civilization. As I walked past the sign, I wondered if the town motto was "What's that smell?" ("It's Rettenegg!")

Eventually I got back to the hotel bar, so all is well that ends well.

Some people obey all signs — no matter what they say. Later on the same trip, we were staying with a bicycle tour group in the little Austrian village of Baden bei Wien when I decided to go for a walk next to the lovely river located just behind our hotel.

Imagine my surprise when I saw our tour friend Susan sitting cross-legged on a big rock in the middle of the river! I waved, but she didn't wave back. I wondered why, but as I got closer I noticed that her eyes were closed.

Then I understood why. On the side of the rock, painted in foot-tall letters, was the word "Meditate." She apparently took that as a direct order, waded out to the rock and sat down and began meditating. She is Canadian, but still.

The problem with so many signs is that people quickly become overloaded and stop reading — or even seeing them. For example, one of my pet peeves (and believe me, that list gets longer by the minute!) is any business that doesn't fully unlock its doors. It's frustrating to approach a store or business only to discover that one half of its entry is locked shut. Usually the way I make this discovery is by trial and error. Depending on whether or not I guess correctly, and how forcefully I pull, I will either blithely enter the business or I will jerk my arm out of its shoulder socket.

That's bad enough, but the greater indignity is having these doors labeled "Push" and "Pull" — and doing just the opposite. This was the subject of a famous Garry Larson cartoon, in which a boy is seen *pulling* on a door at the "School for the Gifted" that is clearly labeled "Push."

Been there, done that.

I do make exceptions for anything that makes me laugh, so for "research" for this chapter, I Googled "funny signs" to see if I could find other signs that would make me laugh.

Well! The next time you feel depressed, you should do the same thing. Here are a few of my favorites:

• Cocktail lounge, Norway: "Ladies are Requested Not to have Children in the Bar"

- Hotel in Acapulco: "The Manager has Personally Passed All the Water Served Here"

- Hotel lobby, Bucharest: "The lift is being fixed for the next day. During that time we regret that you will be unbearable."

- Nairobi restaurant: "Customers who find our waitresses rude ought to see the manager."

- Restaurant window: "Don't stand there and be hungry. Come on in and get fed up."

- Supermarket, Hong Kong: "For your convenience, we recommend courteous, efficient self-service."

- Paris dress shop: "Dresses for street walking."

- Hotel in Zurich: "Because of the impropriety of entertaining guests of the opposite sex in the bedroom, is it suggested that the lobby be used for this purpose."

- Hong Kong tailor: "Ladies may have a fit upstairs."

- Bangkok dry cleaner: "Drop your trousers here for best results."

- Advertisement for a Hong Kong dentist: "Teeth extracted by the latest Methodists."

•   Instructions for a soap bubble gun: "While solution is not toxic it will not make child edible."

•   Japanese hotel room: "Please to bathe inside the tub."

•   Belgrade hotel elevator: "To move the cabin, push button for wishing floor. If the cabin should enter more persons, each one should press a number of wishing floor. Driving is then going alphabetically by national order."

•   Athens hotel: "Visitors are expected to complain at the office between the hours of 9 and 11 A.M. daily."

Okay, so now we have established that I dislike signs — unless they make me laugh. But you will accuse me of hypocritical behavior if you visit our home and use our guest bathroom. There you will find neatly rolled hand towels in a basket with a little sign that says, *"You may place your soiled hand towel in the container in the cabinet below. Thank you."*

How's that for classy? It was my idea, of course. Brad was appalled and said, "What did you think they'd do with the towel — take it home? Throw it in the trash? Flush it down the toilet?"

"No," I said, rolling my eyes. "People won't know there is a *container* for the towels unless we tell them — and a civilized person wouldn't think of opening a cabinet door without being invited to do so.

"And," I continued, "you wouldn't expect me to hang out next to the bathroom door to hand them a towel as they exit the bathroom, would you? So the only obvious solution is a sign."

Now it was his turn to roll his eyes. I swear there are some days when we just sit around rolling our eyes at each other.

There ought to be a sign.

Cara Cares

I have a thing for my dental hygienist, whose name is Cara.

Don't worry — Brad likes her, too — but not just because she is cute and has a perky personality. She also does a great job of cleaning our teeth.

Well, that may be why Brad likes her. I like her because she laughs at everything I say.

If I were a comedian (and contrary to popular opinion, that is not what I want to be) I'd want Cara in the audience simply because she is so easily amused. Early on in our relationship (hygienist/patient) she asked me if I "floss." It should be noted that she had half her arm in my mouth at the time.

See what I mean? Hysterical!

"Certainly not," I replied. (Or, more accurately, "Thurtanlay thnot.") "That's what I pay you to do."

Evidently she thought I was kidding because she laughed and laughed at my answer. But I knew it was only a matter of time — and excavation — before she discovered I was serious.

Cara is special because I haven't had the best of luck

with people in the dental profession. When I was in my early twenties, my dentist and his wife invited me to their house to "get to know them better." Huh? From the way they said it I got the impression we weren't going to be playing dominoes, so I declined. He must not have been too offended, though: after that he gave me so much nitrous oxide I laughed for the rest of the week.

Another dentist became one of my best friends (and is to this day), but several years ago he moved to another town, leaving me dentist-less and friend-less. At my last appointment with him I ordered him to pull all my teeth and give me false teeth so I could mail them back and forth when necessary. (He refused and he eventually came to his senses and moved back to our hometown.)

Readers of my previous book *The Pillow Goes Under Your Head* will recall the dentist who found my crown in the trashcan and popped it right into my mouth. (He is no longer my dentist.)

My current dentist is young, cute and g-a-y. I told Brad we should take turns pulling our own teeth just to give us an excuse to see him.

But as cute as he is, it is the aforementioned hygienist Cara who has won my heart (to say nothing of my molars.)

Until last week, that is.

It is true that nobody wants to hear about another person's physical infirmities, but that doesn't stop people from telling me anyway and it won't stop me from telling you! Mine are treated, as yours may be, with modern medicine — which is to say, pharmaceuticals. Why? Because of those nice people on television. You know: that sweet couple who take baths together — in separate tubs — outdoors! I probably don't need any of the drugs

I take on a daily basis, but I feel it is my duty to take them to keep *Jeopardy!* on the air.

The truth is, I take four pills each day: one is for high cholesterol (who knew French fries are bad for you!?) and the others are for high blood pressure. So what if the pills add only a week or two to my life! What could be better than tacking a few weeks onto your life when you're 90 or 100 years old?

The downside is, well, the downside.

No, not that.

The most noticeable side-effect of my drug regimen is euphemistically called "dry mouth."

So, naturally, when Cara asked me about my current dental health (I don't why she asks — it seems to me she could just *look*) I said, "Well, I have this terrible dry mouth...."

"What do you mean?" she asked, in what I can only assume was a further attempt to be funny.

"Well, it's like this," I said. "I often wake up at one or two in the morning feeling like somebody has just finished swabbing my mouth out with a sponge, then blotted it with gauze, then stuffed a Turkish towel in, then aimed a hair dryer inside, then sanded the inside of my cheeks with #2 grade sandpaper, then...."

"Oh, dry mouth," she said.

Then without missing a beat she reaches into the cabinet where she keeps the free toothbrushes and little samples of dental floss and pulls out a package of — pills! "Why don't you try these," she says. "Some of my patients say they really work."

The pills, as it turns out, aren't pills at all but tablets. They are to be taken two at a time, by inserting them in the space between your teeth and your cheek on each side of your mouth. You are then instructed to leave them there *all night* where they magically create slobber. (That isn't the medical term, by the way.) Unfortunately, by morning you will also discover they have permanently bonded to your teeth.

If you want to know what this feels like, take two breath mints, coat them with SuperGlue and paste them to your teeth. There! Isn't that nice? Better yet, just find a squirrel whose cheeks are stuffed full of nuts and ask him what it feels like.

It is somewhat disconcerting that the tablets come with the ominous instruction, "Do Not Swallow." Huh? How, exactly, do I accomplish that? My mouth does its own thing while I'm asleep (see: "Snoring, Rex") — so how do I keep it from swallowing these things? It's all I can do to keep from swallowing my pillow.

But so far, so good — knock on wood. I haven't swallowed them yet, and when I wake up in the morning I don't have dry mouth! Rather, I have a veritable terrarium of vegetation in my mouth — slimy stuff that feels like the forest floor when it is covered with slick green lichen.

And I give Cara all the credit.

More About Cara

Never in my wildest dreams did I think I would end up getting most of my material for this book from my dental hygienist, but that seems to be what's happening.

Since writing the previous chapter I have had another appointment to have my teeth cleaned. Time to see Cara again — who, for the record, is about the same age as my daughter.

We exchanged the usual pleasantries:

She: "Have you been flossing?"

Me: "No."

She: "Why not?"

Me: "Because."

Then I asked her about her sons who are apparently growing by leaps and bounds. ("You feed 'em, they grow.") And then I settled in for the latest update on her extended family — which, truth be known, is the only reason I come to the dentist.

Cara, you see, is from Michigan, but she sounds like she's from Wisconsin and behaves like she's from Canada. (Remember, I love Canadians.) In other words, she's really, really, really (add "really" 20 more here) *nice*.

Maybe too nice.

Yesterday she told me a story about a trip back to Michigan a few years ago to see her family. During her visit, she went to the local gas station and after she'd finished filling up, a strange man approached her from the sidewalk.

"Would you like some candy?" he asked.

Normally, my jaw would have dropped open upon hearing such an outrageous question, but it was already open — with Cara's fist inside it.

Observing the shock in my eyes — I probably looked like a Margaret Keane drawing — she continued. "Yes, he did. And when I said, 'Oh, no thank you,' he said, 'Do you like kisses?' and I had to tell him 'No thank you,' again!"

Upon hearing this, I made her take her hand out of my mouth.

"You did not!" I exclaimed, my parenting hackles fully up. "Cara, you must learn not to even acknowledge such an inappropriate question, much less respond to it! He was obviously coming on to you and you should have put him in his place!"

"Oh," she said, sounding somewhat puzzled by my stridency. "You may be right. When I got back to my relative's house, I told my cousin what had happened and she said, 'Oh, that fool is there all the time offering people candy. I told him 'No' once and he threw the candy at me and a piece hit me right in the forehead!'"

Somehow, in Cara's mind, that was just about the most horrible thing a strange man could have done to a young woman alone at the filling station: throw a piece of candy at her. I briefly thought about telling her what else could have happened, followed by a lecture about personal safety, etc., but I decided it was unfair for me to try to parent her.

But that story launched a discussion of the crazy things people say and do and it was now my turn to shock her.

I told her a story that had happened only a few days earlier, when I was shopping at our local supermarket. It was early in the morning — no later than 9 o'clock — and I had a full cart. The checker — or clerk, depending on where you're from — was new to me, whereas most of them know me by name.

Or at least I thought they knew me by name because during several previous visits I would simply walk through the front doors and hear my name being announced over the loud speaker. And, while it's true that we spend an enormous sum of money on groceries each week, I was amazed that they would make such a big deal out of my arrival.

Then I made the mistake of commenting on it to one of the cashiers.

"I can't tell you how flattering it is to hear my name announced when I walk into your store," I told her.

She was momentarily taken aback then put two and two together. Smiling somewhat sheepishly, she said, "Oh. I'm afraid you may have misunderstood. Our manager's name is Rex. They were probably paging him…"

Ouch. Ego check.

But on this particular morning, I didn't recognize the cashier and I knew she didn't know me, so you can imagine my surprise when out of the clear blue she looked me right in the eye and said, "Are you sober?"

Did I mention that this was before 9 o'clock in the morning?

"I beg your pardon," I said, arching my eyebrows appropriately. "You do realize it's not even noon yet. Why wouldn't I be sober — and while we're at it, I must say I'm shocked that you would even ask me such a question!"

At this, she stopping punching the keys on her cash register and smiled as she said, slowly and clearly, "I'm sorry. I didn't ask if you are sober — I asked if you are a *snowbird.*"

(For those of you who don't live in a resort climate, a snowbird is someone who lives elsewhere but spends winter in a sunny locale.)

Needless to say, I burst out laughing at the checker (and myself) and Cara burst out laughing when I retold the story.

I suppose it could have been worse. That cashier could have thrown a piece of candy at me.

If It's Thursday I Can't Hear You

It is a well-known fact that old people are creatures of habit. That group of old guys you saw down at the coffee shop Tuesday morning? Go back next Tuesday. I'll bet they'll be there again.

My dear stepmother, during the last thirty years of her life, called me every Sunday morning at 10 a.m. Not 9:45, mind you, or 10:05. Exactly at 10 o'clock. I never had to set an alarm clock on Sunday morning because I knew I would be awakened by a ringing telephone. (I once asked if she would mind calling a bit later, say at noon, and she said, "No, I think 10 o'clock works better for me....")

Now that I have joined the ranks of the aged, I can relate.

For us, laundry is done on Monday, as God ordained.

Tuesdays the lawn is 'mowed and blowed' — by an army of lawn personnel armed with the loudest mowers and blowers you've ever heard.

The dry cleaning is picked up on Wednesdays and, as compensation, includes a trip to Starbucks.

Grocery shopping is scheduled for Friday morning —

and don't ask me why, since it is one of the busiest days of the week in a grocery store.

The weekends are when we get wild and wacky — sometimes sleeping as late as 6 a.m. And then it's back to our regular routine.

Haircuts are a bit trickier, because they don't fall on the same day, and it makes me furious that my hair isn't more dependable. But we schedule our haircuts for every third Monday — and God help the hairs that grow too slowly, they're getting cut anyway.

But it is our weirdest habit that inspired the title of this book.

On a Thursday morning about a year ago, just after we'd finished eating breakfast and Brad was about to put the dishes in the dishwasher (I'm not allowed to load the dishwasher because he says I "don't know how"), he asked me if I would do him a favor. It never occurred to me to ask what the favor was — he never asks for anything — so of course I said yes.

He handed me a little green plastic bottle. "Please put just five drops — exactly five — from this little bottle into each of my ears."

"Say what? You want me to clean your ears?" I can't be trusted to clean the dishes but apparently his ears are up for grabs.

"In a manner of speaking...yes...the doctor told me it will keep wax from building up."

Well, okay. I'm not about to stand in the way of Brad's clean ear goals, so I took the little bottle from him and asked where he wanted to conduct this grooming task.

By way of explanation, he put his head down on the breakfast bar. Oh. Okay. But seeing his head lying there in front of me reminded me of a luncheon I once attended in Seville, Spain, where the waiter placed a platter on the table in front of me with the entire head of a pig on it. For a split second I wondered what Brad would look like if I popped a small apple into his mouth.

As I put the drops in I counted to myself to make sure I got exactly five: *'One...two...three...four...five...SIX!'* I couldn't help it — it came out before I could tip the little bottle back into its upright position. Now what!?! Will that extra drop eat through his eardrum like acid?

I must have made a small noise because he said, "What's wrong?"

"Nothing," I lied. "Turn your head over." I was extra vigilant on this particular ear and it received only the prescribed five drops, but I will always wonder if he has slightly better hearing in that other ear because of that extra drop.

"Is that it?" I asked.

"Yep. That's all there is to it. Thank you."

And with that we began a tradition that continues to this day (provided you are reading this book on a Thursday.)

But a few months ago it occurred to me that he was having all the fun. What about *my* ears? For all I knew, I could have a regular candle factory in the middle of my head. Then I remembered several years ago when I thought I had spontaneously gone deaf and made an emergency trip to my doctor's office without even calling ahead for an appointment. The receptionist looked at me like I'd lost my mind. "I'm sorry, Mr. John, but you'll need an appointment."

"What?" I said, bellowing, since I couldn't hear myself.

She repeated herself.

"What?" I yelled. "I've lost my hearing."

Exasperated, she got up and fetched the doctor. He decided to see me — without an appointment (call *Ripley's Believe it or Not!*) — and I was escorted into a little exam room where I was told to take off my shirt.

"What?" I said, not believing what I'd heard — although I didn't actually hear it, or at least not clearly.

The nurse acted out what she wanted me to do — although she didn't take her shirt off, thankfully.

I said, "What?" again — this time with some astonishment. "It's my ears we're worried about — not my pecs!" I screamed.

She smiled patronizingly and I think she said something about not wanting to soil my clothes.

So I took my shirt off and put on the backwards gown she offered.

A stainless steel pan was brought out which looked suspiciously like a doggie dish. A few instruments were lined up on a tray table on wheels. "Dear God," I thought, "they're going to do surgery on me — and I don't even have an appointment!"

Something was poured into each ear and then the doctor stood by and stared at me for a few minutes. The nurse soon lost interest and, I assume, went to lunch.

Finally the doctor held the dog dish under my right ear and plunged one of his instruments into my ear. (In retelling this story at that time I said it was an electric drill, but it really wasn't.) In less than a second I heard the loud CLANK of something falling in the dog dish — a half-dollar, maybe? He held it in front of my face like I might want a closer look, which I most certainly did not.

"What is it?" I shouted.

"It's what was keeping you from hearing," he said proudly, as though he'd just witnessed a major medical breakthrough.

I was appalled of course and resolved to change doctors, since I obviously couldn't continue going to a doctor who thought I had such poor hygienic habits that I would jeopardize my own hearing.

But that was then, and this is now.

Thanks to Brad, I'm now in on the action too. I do him, then he does me — and that's how Thursday has officially become Ear Cleaning Day at our house.

So, if you happen to be at our house on Thursday morning, don't be alarmed if instead of bowing our heads to say Grace, we tip them to the side.

When Old McDonald is Your Decorator

Lots of us have hobbies.

Some people are stamp collectors, for example…no, that can't be right. I've never met anybody in my life who collects stamps. What's the point? If the stamps are unused, it's not like you can use them on an email or text message, and if they're already cancelled, well, isn't that like a used concert ticket? You ain't gonna see the show a second time!

I asked Brad about this. "Maybe they collect them for their artistic value. Have you ever looked at some of the artwork on today's stamps?"

Well, no. I prefer artwork that doesn't require a magnifying glass.

So I started doing a little research on stamp collecting and — wouldn't you know — there are 20 million stamp collectors in China alone!

After reading a draft of this book, our neighbor Lois told me that her father collected stamps his whole life — and ended up with *eight* six-foot storage lockers filled with binders of *stamps!* With all due respect to Lois, I thought that sounded crazy until she told me the rest of the story:

when he retired he sold *some* of his stamps and bought a new car!

So much for my (former) belief that stamp collecting "doesn't make any sense!"

And now I have discovered that a single stamp — a British Guiana One-Cent Magenta, to be exact — sold at auction for *nine and a half million dollars.* I stand corrected. Everybody should be collecting stamps. In fact, I plan to start collecting stamps immediately. (To help me get started, please don't hesitate to send me a letter by U.S. Mail. Be sure to put a British Guiana One- Cent Magenta in the top right-hand corner.)

As a kid I had mostly stupid hobbies. Like most boys my age I once received a wood-burning kit for Christmas and set about making burned wood items for all my friends and loved ones. To the best of my knowledge, none of these *objets d'art* survives today. But I still can't get that smell out of my brain. I do think it's odd that a nine-year old kid would be given something to play with that could have caused permanent scars — or burned the house down. I would probably have gotten around to both if I could have stood the smell.

I also remember getting a paint-by-number kit but that didn't work out either. After I painstakingly dabbed the paint into each little numbered area as per the instructions, I couldn't tell which was the top of the picture and which was the bottom. Or what the picture was. I declared it a work of art nonetheless and vaguely recall propping it up on the milk box on our front porch with a sign attached that said 50¢. When the mailman showed up I asked if he wanted to buy it. He just shook his head and shot me a strange look before continuing on his way. About ten minutes later my friend Olaf came charging up on his bike and said, "C'mon! The mailman says there's a strange kid on the porch down the block. Let's go find him!"

Photography was a short-lived hobby, too. My grandmother gave me an Ansco Shur Shot Box Camera which, looking back, was so simple I could probably have made it myself out of burned wood. I wish I'd kept that camera because today it would probably be a valuable antique.

(Strike that. I just found one on E-Bay with a starting bid of $14.99.)

I was briefly interested in trains — it was required in the Boy Manual when I was growing up. I wanted an American Flyer — they were sleek and black and silver and ran on two rails, just like, well…a train.

But instead my parents gave me a Lionel Train Set, which was all wrong. The cars were big enough to hold a hamster and, worst of all, they rode on three rails. Three! Why? What train (besides the subway) has three rails? That ruined it for me. That and the fact the kit came with only enough track to make a small circle. There's only so much thrill a kid can get out of watching a train go round and round and round and round. It made me want to get out my wood burning kit and set something on fire.

Believe it or not, I recently thought of resurrecting my train hobby — or at least I told Brad I was thinking about it just to see the look of horror on his face. We had been invited to tour a home in our neighborhood in which the owner (a Medicare-eligible adult) had permanently installed train tracks on a shelf that ran around the perimeter of every room in his house. The shelf was about a foot below the ceiling so you couldn't really see the action up close, but if you stepped back into the room you could follow the train as it raced along the walls of the living room before departing for the bedrooms, bathrooms and kitchen, eventually making its way back to the living room. Woo! Woo! I could just imagine if we had such a set-up in our house. Me, calling Brad on my cellphone: "We seem to be out of toilet paper in this bathroom. Will you please put a roll on the next train out of the pantry?"

Some of my friends have wonderful, interesting hobbies. My friend Greg, for example, has saved every airline ticket inside its *ticket jacket* for every trip he's ever taken. He has a stack at least three feet tall — in chronological order! When the airlines stopped using paper tickets, he found a website where he could purchase ticket jackets so he could continue his hobby. There's obviously something wrong with him. I'd tell him to talk to a doctor — but he is one!

Another friend — or former friend, I should say — has the nasty little habit of "collecting" dinner plates. Not from the homes of her friends, thankfully. ("Honey, I could have sworn we put out eight dinner plates — what did Melissa eat on, her lap?") No, she stole them from restaurants! And by restaurants, I don't mean Denny's where I doubt the dinner plates are particularly collectable. Her collection comprises charger plates (the plate that is already on the table when you arrive) from some of the most expensive restaurants in the world.

I was aware of her collection but didn't really understand how she acquired the plates until we were seated for dinner at the very chic Le Taillevent in the 8th Arrondissement. Le Taillevent features, among other things, a lovely New Year's Eve prix fixe menu at 500 euros *per person, excluding beverages.*

In other words, not cheap.

My friends were treating me (praise the Lord) so I was on my best behavior…until Melissa announced her intentions over cocktails.

"See this here charger plate?" she whispered conspiratorially. (She's from Texas, which explains the 'this here.')

"Yes," I said cheerfully. "It's lovely, isn't it?"

"Well, I'm going to take it home!"

"Oh?" I said, not quite understanding what she was getting at. "They actually sell their china?"

"Oh no!" she said. "We already tried that and they told us no in no uncertain terms. They say they have *never* sold their china and it's very hard to replace, blah blah blah."

"And…?" I said, as the light slowly dawned.

At that she picked up her gigantic Hermes bag from the seat of the banquette and said, "That's why I brought this!"

"You are *not* going to steal that plate, Melissa. I forbid it. I'm not going to end up in some French jail tonight!"

"Don't be silly. They'll never know!"

I wasn't having it. It was wrong and she knew it. I knew it. Anybody with any brains would know it.

I waited a short while and excused myself to go to the men's room. On my way, I snagged the maitre d' and somehow impressed on him how important it was for me to be able to buy one of their charger plates, and could he please just this once make an exception…and I would be happy to pay any price he might ask…."

He looked me squarely in the eye and said, "For you, Monsieur, we will make an exception. I will take care of it." I gave him all my cash and returned to my seat.

At the end of the meal, over dessert, as Melissa was getting ready to snatch one of the charger plates from the vacant table next to us, a waiter appeared with a large gift bag. Inside was a beautifully wrapped box containing one of the charger plates.

I love the French.

But I never saw Melissa again.

There are other less criminal hobbies that are just as weird. My late stepmother, may she rest in peace, collected butter tubs. Not lovely little glass pieces on which you would place a cube of butter but, rather, the plastic tubs that margarine is sold in. When she died we found at least 1,000 of them in the basement.

If I ever had a hobby that might "take," I suppose it would be interior design. I know, that's a bit *cliché*. But I could have chosen flower-arranging or hair-dressing, couldn't I?

But I admit that I like HGTV and sometimes I will turn it on just to annoy Brad. He prefers silence to watching television. I think he went to too many silent movies as a child.

Interestingly enough, I've learned a lot from those TV shows — but mostly I haven't learned *what* to do so much as what *not* to do — which, simply put, is this: *don't try to impose your so-called taste on everybody else.*

Forty years ago, before cable TV had been invented — much less "The Property Brothers" — I bought a house and proceeded to paint and carpet every room a different color. My wife and I did all the work ourselves and we were quite proud of our efforts. But when we invited one of our more sophisticated friends over to see our handiwork, I asked him what he thought, and his reply was sharp and to the point: "Too many colors. You should have used one carpet color to tie the rooms together."

I don't remember what he said after that because I instantly hated him. In fact, I honestly don't even remember his name anymore. (So, if you're reading this, What's Your Name, I hope you've learned some tact by now. Oh, and you'll be happy to know that I have always used the same carpet throughout every home I've owned from that day to this!)

Let's face it: taste is subjective. Over the years I've learned that I personally may not like a particular decor, but that doesn't mean it's not well done. My taste leans towards contemporary, but many of our friends like more traditional styles — and I love their homes. I've been in sumptuous homes that I wouldn't choose for myself, but I still like them because they're nicely done. We don't all have to have the same taste, do we?

Which obviously brings us to the subject of barn doors.

Our TV must have been on the blink the day they told everybody to start remodeling with barn doors, but I don't think I've been in a home or business in the past year that hasn't featured a door with the hanging hardware clearly visible. As I write this, I am sitting in a lovely apartment in San Clemente, California. You can look out any window and see a beautiful expanse of Pacific Ocean. You can also walk down the hall and, without any effort at all, see everything that's happening inside the bathroom — even though the door is "closed"! That's because the door is hung on the outside of the opening and features a two-inch gap. Stylish? Yes! But if we invite guests over, I bet they'll want to stuff towels in the cracks (of the door) for some privacy.

Brad, who coined the expression "Early Olive Garden" to describe a decorating style that favors lots of earth tones, big dark ceiling beams and ornate wrought-iron chandeliers, refers to the decorating style of any home featuring more than a half-dozen barn doors as "Early Dust Bowl" — or, if he's feeling particularly feisty, "Old MacDonald's Other Farm."

Ouch. I think he needs to start collecting stamps.

Lucky Bites

I'm not a gambler...anymore. Oh, I never was, really
—— and all it took was one particularly unlucky trip to
Las Vegas to cure me for good.

That and Brad, that is.

If and when we travel through Las Vegas, either on
our way in or out of California, he has been known to
allow me twenty dollars for the "slots." Slot machines, as
everybody knows, are simply an easy way to pass the
time. Sort of like sitting on the sofa changing the TV
channels with a remote control, only every time you
change the channel it costs you twenty-five cents.

(Memo to self: patent that as a new invention.)

Some people (like my friend Christine) have been
known to entertain themselves for hours just sitting at a
slot machine, slowly throwing their money away. And
get this: Christine does it *a penny at a time!* For all I know,
she's at the same slot machine where I left her sitting at a
few years ago, still trying to get rid of that dollar.

My personal record for making that twenty dollars
Brad gives me last "as long as possible" is about eighteen

minutes.

But then there's the lottery.

When the lottery first came to Colorado, it was in the form of scratch-off tickets. It was introduced with a PR blitz befitting a circus or the moon landing. But I ignored it all, because I knew better. I knew if I started buying lottery tickets, it would only be a short time 'til I lost my car, my house, my job, and my first-born child (bye-bye, Elisabeth! I love you!).

But then I reasoned if I *did* lose my house and car, I wouldn't have a place to keep my kids anyway, so why not buy just one ticket?

(I admit this is strange logic, but it worked at the time. Amazing how that works, isn't it — no matter how silly it sounds in retrospect, it makes perfect sense if you want to do something.)

So I bought a ticket. One ticket. I'll never forget standing in line at King Soopers, our big local grocery chain, and telling the clerk I'd like to buy "one of those new lottery tickets." She looked at me like I was crazy since the lottery had already been around for over a year.

When she handed it to me, I said, "How does it work?"

Now she did think I was crazy and was getting ready to grab her intercom ("Mental Health Professional to register four, please…") when a nice lady behind me said, "You just scratch off that silver coating with a penny, dear."

So I did. Right there, in line, with people waiting behind me. If it was to be the only time I bought a lottery ticket, I wanted to share the experience with those around me. (To be honest, they didn't seem as excited as I thought they should be.)

And wouldn't you know: my first lottery ticket won $500!

Well. Let's just guess how long it took them to get that $500 back. (Hint: about as long as it takes to say "I'm an idiot.")

But losing that $500 almost as quickly as I'd won it provided a cure of sorts. I was annoyed that I'd just thrown it away. So now, years later, I rarely buy lottery tickets — and only when the jackpot exceeds $500 million. (Less than $500 million? Who needs it, right?)

Not long ago I happened to read that the jackpot had climbed to $1.6 *billion* of which, after taking the "cash option" (half) and paying taxes (also half) I'd have approximately $400 million *left*. I could live with that.

I didn't win, of course — and now I want my two dollars back.

Several months earlier, for a different mega-drawing, the winning numbers came from a ticket purchased in Menifee, California — which happens to be in the same county in which I live! In other words, I was *this close!*

(To get the full impact of that last sentence, put your index finger and thumb together and read the sentence again. See?)

But here's the thing. They announced the numbers, told where the ticket was purchased, and then....nada. A week later the winner still hadn't come forward!

I don't know about you, but if I'd won that jackpot I would have been on the first limo headed to Lottery Headquarters to collect my dough. Six days? I'd have been there in six hours — before the lottery people spent it on something else — like "education," which is where California lottery funds end up. Ha! Like education is all that important! (Says the person who just threw away two dollars on a slip of paper with six numbers written on it.)

In the same article, it was reported that winners often take their time before claiming the money. Another California couple took more than six months to claim their share another $1.586 *billion* jackpot.

Now that's just crazy. What if they'd lost the ticket in that period of time? I'd love to have heard the conversation in that house.

"I'm sure I gave it to you, honey…."

"No, I don't think so…."

"Sure I did. Remember, I used the back to write down a couple of things you needed to pick up at the grocery store…."

So, here's today's helpful hint. You only have one year to claim your lottery winnings. If you miss it by just one day, you're…wait for it…*out of luck.*

Can you imagine how you would feel if you waited a year and a day — and missed out on your big payoff? Talk about a bad day!

We've already determined that I am either very lucky (the $500 scratch- off) or very unlucky (the $2 worthless PowerBall ticket) but the truth is, I'm probably neither — because I'm pretty sure luck is a made-up concept. As some wag said, "Depend on a rabbit's foot if you will, but remember, it didn't work for the rabbit!"

And yet, I can't help thinking about all the things that have happened to me that might be labeled as "lucky"…

…like when I'm driving down the street and all the red lights turn green just as I approach them;

…or when I drop a piece of toast on the floor and it

lands jelly-side up (That's just crazy. I've never dropped a piece of toast on the floor on my life — and I don't eat jelly);

...or when I left my pants in some random French village and they eventually find their way to a different hotel in a different village a week later;

...or I opened a clamshell package of 50 Gillette razor blades today (from Costco; guess who bought them) and didn't require a trip to the emergency room;

...or I've had the Heimlich maneuver performed on me *two times* in different restaurants and I'm still alive to tell about it;

...or I've learned to take smaller bites.

On second thought, maybe I am pretty lucky.

Walk, Santa Claus, Walk!

This chapter was written months ago. Meanwhile, Christmas has come and gone and it's time for another one. My son and daughter-in-law and my youngest granddaughter will be spending the holidays with us, so we have decided to forego our standard policy known as "Bah Humbug" and instituted a new one called "Deck the Halls."

In other words, we got a Christmas tree. If you read my previous book *The Pillow Goes Under Your Head* you know that choosing — and transporting — a Christmas tree isn't my strong suit. But, we got it done, and decorated, and I thought the end result was worth the effort.

As I stood admiring our work, I said, "I think our house looks quite festive."

To which Brad replied, "Infested with what!?"

Therein lies the problem. We are both becoming increasingly hearing-impaired.

We have subsequently decided there are several options available to us:

    1.   Hearing aids (or, as they are euphemistically

referred to, "devices").

2. Surgery. There isn't a surgery available for our particular affliction, but I wanted bunion surgery so I put surgery on the list. (We could ignore our hearing problems, I reasoned, but at least my feet wouldn't hurt.)

3. Increasing the volume of everybody and everything around us. Turning up the TV would be the easy part; getting other people to yell at us when they wanted us to hear something posed more of a challenge.

"It's not just the volume," Brad said. "I can hear people when they speak clearly." And he can. In fact, we got him those hearing devices but he wears them only a fraction of the time, like when we're going to restaurants, movies, or the homes of soft-spoken friends — a rarity, to be sure.

I realized he had unwittingly given me a brilliant idea. I designed a T- shirt and had it printed and suggested he wear it everywhere we go. What do you think it says?

If you guessed, "I'm deaf as a post," you're wrong.

"HEARING CHALLENGED"? Wrong again.

It says, in simple plain lettering, "Please stop mumbling."

I think it may be working, too, but I'm sick of seeing him in that shirt. I'm going to have another T-shirt made, for myself, that says "Please get a new shirt."

Don't tell the hearing device industry, but I don't think impairment is as much of a problem as mumbling is. And everybody does it now, not just recalcitrant teenagers.

My friend Kurt used to be the fitness director at our club and I loved to go workout when Kurt was on duty because I could count on him for a good thirty-minute conversation which meant thirty fewer minutes to work out!   One day he told me a funny story about his partner, Ivan, who had just told him on the phone that the weather person on TV was predicting temperatures of "150 degrees."

"What!" Kurt exclaimed. "That's impossible!"

"No it isn't," Ivan countered. "Actually, she said 150 to 180 degrees."

"Ivan," Kurt said patiently, "It has never been that hot in Palm Springs. Never!" But then Kurt, never forgetting for a moment that his husband is a native Italian, remembered he sometimes confused words like "kitchen" and "chicken." Could this be another one of those moments, or were we truly on the verge of the apocalypse? That sexy Italian accent had been know to work for and against Ivan.

But, upon further checking, sure enough — the prediction was for temperatures of *115 to 118* — quite a difference from 150 and 180, but still nothing to feel relieved about. (See "Warming , Global.")

Interestingly, fifteen and fifty *do* sound similar if you say them quickly, drop the "n" at the end and with an Italian accent.   In other words, if Ivan says it.

It can't be defined as mumbling if it involves somebody for whom English isn't the primary language.

Or can it?

We went to Venice a few years ago after Brad finished two weeks — and 500 miles — of bicycling in the Alps. To get there, we had to take a train from Castelfranco, Italy across the bridge to Venice, approximately 30 minutes.

When we arrived, Brad called for a taxi. And by taxi,

of course, I mean "boat."

As the driver (sailor?) was tossing our two bags onto the boat ("Thank you for not missing!") I had the presence of mind to ask him how much the fare would be to our hotel, which I knew was within swimming distance — although an inconvenient swim when towing two big bags.

"How much?" I said.

"Fifblah euros," he replied, his mouth apparently full of marbles.

"I'm sorry — how much?" I asked.

"Fifblah euros," he repeated.

"Fifteen?" I asked.

"Yes, fifblah," he said.

So, when we reached the hotel three minutes later, I handed him three five-euro notes. He looked at them, and then at me, before announcing in perfect boarding school English, "*Not fifteen. FIFTY.*"

And what do we learn from that, boys and girls? That foreigners are just as guilty as Americans when it comes to mumbling.

But wait — there's more! Now it's not only people who mumble, but inanimate objects do, too!

Proof: we once spent July in the darling little town of Sebastopol, California — about 60 miles north of San Francisco. While walking downtown one day we encountered what appeared to be your standard stoplight at a street corner, complete with a push-button to signal the "walk" light.

I pushed it.

We waited.

In a moment we heard a faint voice which appeared to be coming out of the button itself. We looked at it, then looked at each other and said, "Wha...?"

In a moment, we heard it again — and it was coming out of the button! Brad quickly leaned over to see if he could hear the words, at which time I helpfully observed, "You look like you're trying to push that button with your ear."

But then we heard it again. The word "walk" was clear as a bell, but it was followed by a few more metallic sounds that we simply could not make out.

So what did we do? Did we shrug our shoulders and walk on? Nooooo! We stood there through three more cycles of the light as it said whatever it was it was saying over and over again.

By this time I had knelt in front of the pole. "You look like you're licking that button," Brad said in an obvious attempt to pay me back.

Mystified, I said, "I think it keeps saying...'Walk, Santa Claus. Walk!'"

But that would be stupid, since it was July. Looking back, it would have been stupid no matter what month it was.

"That makes no sense," Brad offered helpfully.

"No, but I think that's what it's saying."

The next day, we found ourselves on the same corner, at the same light — Brad again trying to push the button with his ear while I licked the pole.

Once again, that stupid button kept saying, "Walk, Santa Claus. Walk!"

Eventually we decided that what it was really *mumbling* was, "Walk! Signal is on! Walk!" This made about as much sense as "Walk, Santa Claus," but we decided to drop it and just cross the street, since we were on our way to pick up some running shoes I had seen on sale.

"How much are they?" Brad wanted to know.

"Just fifblah dollars," I said, earning a puzzled look from him in return.

But it's not my fault. He wasn't wearing his T-shirt.

Quest for the Holy Sofa

We have friends who count in years how long they have been together as a couple.

That's quaint, but we have a better way. We count the number of sofas we have owned together. I swear my next anniversary card to Brad is going to say, "Happy Third Anniversary!" because that's how long we have owned our current sofa — and that's a record for us.

Let's quickly review. There were the sofas we each owned when we first met. His was some futon-looking thing on a plywood-looking frame that you'd expect to find in Boulder, which was where he lived at the time. It went straight to Goodwill.

I owned two sofas at the time — a red one and a green — which wasn't as hideous as it sounds since they were kept in separate rooms so people wouldn't think Santa's elves had done my decorating.

The green sofa was olive colored and held only two people, so we ditched that one and started using the red one — a sectional — exclusively.

One evening I watched something on TV that had a

lot of blood and guts in it and the next morning I was convinced the red sofa was giving me nightmares. "Hello, Goodwill…?"

Then we moved in together and bought a nice new sofa at Pottery Barn. It had a tweedy fabric and wooden arms and was beautiful to look at. Sitting? Not so much. It was harder than a church pew and made you feel like your mother had just ordered you to "Sit up straight!" My posture on that sofa was so perfect I was tempted to balance a book on my head.

We gave that sofa to our housekeeper who probably gave it to Goodwill.

Next was a sectional we inherited when we bought a furnished condo in California.

"Do you think you'll be able to live with this furniture?" Brad asked as we were trying to decide whether to buy it?

"Sure!" I lied, wondering where the nearest Goodwill was.

I don't even remember what came next except that it was so unsatisfactory we promptly gave it to the gardener who deserved punishment because he let some of our bushes die: "Take that, you rose killer!"

Our current sofa — number 7, if you've been counting — was specially ordered from a store called Roche-Bobois — pronounced "roash-bo-bwah" if you're French or merely pretentious — and it cost more than my Junior year in college.

I will say this. It is made out of leather so soft and creamy you'd swear it was edible (and may have been at one time, if you catch my drift.)

Before we ordered it — one doesn't just "buy" such a piece, one "orders" it and then waits months for them to produce it — we measured every which way but loose to make sure it would be just the right size. Do you understand? It was made to our exact specifications — except one: its height.

Who measures the height of a chair — or sofa — anyway? Aren't they all basically the same height?

Nay, nay!

This sofa is so low that — and I swear I'm not making this up — we had to cut the legs off our coffee table. Cutting the legs off furniture is clearly a Brad job, since if I were to do it we'd forever be adjusting for "the wobble" — a quarter-inch here…oh now this leg seems a bit short, so let's take off a quarter-inch on this one…and so forth, until the poor piece wouldn't have any legs at all.

The problem with buying a sofa — or any piece of furniture for that matter — is that it must fit the space allocated for it. L-shaped sofas can be problematic because usually there is only one way to place them in the room. Our friends Bruce and Bonnie have discovered this with their extremely comfortable sofa which also happens to be L-shaped.

It's perfect right where it is, offering a stunning view of a golf course and mountains in the background. You wouldn't think of moving it — unless you later wanted to accommodate a piano, which is something they would like to do.

As we sat pondering this dilemma over glasses of Champagne a few weeks ago, Brad came up with what he thought would be a perfect solution: "Turn the sofa this way and put the piano in the middle of the room."

Putting the piano in the middle of the room wouldn't have been a bad idea if you owned, say, a piano bar or if you were in the habit of giving concerts in your living room. If I played the piano like Bruce I would probably put it on a rotating dais with spotlights. But unfortunately Brad's brilliant idea would have left Bruce and Bonnie's guests literally facing the wall.

"Um, I'm not sure our guests would like that," Bonnie offered diplomatically, no doubt wondering if perhaps Brad had had one glass of the bubbly too many.

I came up with a much better alternative, a complicated plan which involved getting rid of their dining room furniture and eating off the coffee table or a picnic cloth spread out on the floor.

Bonnie didn't seem to care for that idea either, as evidenced by the rolling of her eyes.

Frankly, I hope they never get a piano because the current situation requires Bruce to play the piano at our house, which is the only time our piano gets played. We love to invite them to dinner because it means a night of free entertainment. Better yet, Bonnie is an amazing cook and always insists on bringing most of the food. The only things we contribute are a few bottles of wine and a chance to sit on a perfectly uncomfortable sofa in front of a coffee table with sawn-off legs.

How did you like that last chapter? How about this one?

Brad made a strange announcement the other day after we came from watching a movie in the theater in which they showed half-a-dozen commercials before the movie started.

"When I die," he began, which always puts me on edge, "I want two things. First, I want commercials at my funeral."

"Commercials?"

"Yes," he said. "It's a perfect marketing opportunity and if it's done right, it could actually pay for the whole funeral."

"Well, that's not going to happen," I informed him. "So what's the second thing?"

"I think you should pass out a 'Satisfaction Survey.'"

I laughed of course and told him he wouldn't be getting either one and wouldn't even have a funeral as far as I was concerned.

But later I started thinking about the Satisfaction Survey and realized that a funeral is one of the few places we don't have to fill one out.

As best I can recall, this all started for me at Home Depot several years ago when I bought a screwdriver and was handed a paper receipt that stretched all the way to the floor.

"What is this?" I asked, stunned.

"That's your receipt," the clerk replied. (I was going to write "cheerfully replied," but I think we all know better.)

"Yes, but why is it so…long?" I asked. "It's not like a bought 100 screws." (Which of course, would justify a yard-long receipt only if you itemized each one, line-by-line.)

"Oh, this just contains information on how to rate your experience," she replied, still un-cheerfully.

"What experience?" I asked, genuinely mystified.

Now it was her turn to be confused. "Um…buying the screwdriver…?" But, noting my incredulousness, she quickly added, "And you can win $500!"

Thus it began and continues to this day. Did I win the $500? No, and I'll bet nobody else has, either. But, in my defense, it only took the completion of half-a-dozen on-line surveys before I figured out that they are yet another marketing scam.

"Why…" (feigning a Southern accent and batting my eyes) "…I think they may be fiddlin' with me!"

But like marijuana, Home Depot proved to be just an entry-level drug. It wasn't long till I was mainlining the equivalent of heroin — rating restaurants, hotels, shoes, pants, books, movies, basically anything and everything that crossed my path.

They want my opinion? Well, by gosh, I'll give it to them — and then some! I quickly became that guy who, as my ex-mother-in-law used to say, "wouldn't say in few words what could be said in many." (Not that she was one to talk.)

I am beginning to be a bit more judicious in my ratings and now confine myself to something I can do in five stars or less. The unfortunate thing about this is, I now have a tendency to rate everything on a one-to-five star scale.

"How did you sleep last night?" Brad asks.

"About a three."

"Does this stoplight seem unusually long?"

"Maybe a four."

"How was your prostate exam?"

"I'd give it a two."

Isn't this getting out of hand? We recently bought a car and received a ten-page, single-spaced Satisfaction Survey. Ten pages! As far as I'm concerned, they could have asked me two questions and they would know everything I like/don't like about our car:

1. Does it go places? Me: Yes.

2. Is it clean? Me: Yes — well, it was when we got it.

Fine. The rating is 4 Stars. It would have been 5, but it doesn't stay clean, which is annoying.

Oops, make that 3 Stars. I can't get used to the locations of the turn signal and windshield wiper control. True, I live in a community where using a turn signal is considered grandiose, but when I'm feeling important and showy, I don't like squirting water all over the windshield when all I wanted to do was make a left turn.

But it's not just screwdrivers, restaurants and cars.

My own modesty would normally prevent me from bragging about an award I just received, but since you insist I will admit that I am now a Level 5 contributor to TripAdvisor.com. Even more exciting — if you can imagine such a thing — I am a Level 15 Restaurant Expert!

That's all fine and good — who knew that eating out all the time carried such weighty responsibilities — but I'll admit I'm sick of reviewing everything I do.

Or, as Henry IV so aptly put it, "uneasy lies the head that wears a crown."

(When I mentioned this to Brad he said, "Really? Did TripAdvisor.com find a crown big enough for your head?")

As I write this we are in another city where we took an Uber this morning. One of the things we like about Uber and Lyft is that they are both so quick and efficient — and there is no cash involved, so it feels free.

But of course they couldn't leave well enough alone. Now you are invited to rate your driver on a one to five scale. This is relatively easy for me, because my ratings are based simply on whether or not they got me there alive. They did? Five stars!

But then I found out the Uber drivers also rate the customers.

Say what?!?

That's right, or so my friend Jill says. Jill lives in New York City with her girlfriend and an adorable little Shizu.

Jill has lived in New York all her life. Translation: she doesn't take crap from anybody — including Uber drivers. If they take too long to pick her up, they hear about it. If their car is untidy, they hear about it. And, God forbid, if they splash her when they pull up to the curb, well, let's just say they most definitely hear about it.

So, imagine Jill's surprise when she discovered that all

of a sudden Uber drivers seemed to be taking longer to arrive. (More than a New York minute, that is.) Why? she wondered. She could see their little car icons swarming all over the place on her iPhone — so what was taking so long? When she mentioned this dilemma to a co-worker, she was told, "Oh, you probably have a poor rating."

I wish I'd been there for *that* conversation! But after all the sputtering indignity, she got right on the phone and — you guessed it — told Uber what she thought of their rating system!

To her credit, Jill learns quickly. Adopting the persona of a Broadway star, she became sweet as pie overnight and apparently her rating went back up and now she doesn't have to wait more than a split-second ("too long!") for a car.

But now that Jill has told me about the Uber drivers rating customers, for heaven's sakes, I'm not quite so cavalier about how I rate *them*. I've started paying attention so I can grade my drivers fairly and accurately.

Today, for example, the app told me to expect "Joshumel" in four minutes. I spent most of that time wondering what kind of name "Joshumel" was and what his mother could possibly have been thinking. But when he pulled up in his white Prius in exactly four minutes and greeted me with a big smile as he said my name aloud, well, what's not to like? Sure, maybe I would have preferred a different colored car — a cream-colored Bentley, for example — but Joshumel's was clean and smelled like....what was that smell? Baked cookies? Did he have an oven in there? I know you're supposed to bake cookies when you're trying to sell a house, but I've never heard of infusing a car with the scent of freshly-baked cookies. Was he trying to sell me this car? And where, exactly, are the darn cookies? I want one!

"Joshumel, it smells like cookies in here…," I finally said, hoping he would take the hint and offer me one.

"Yes!" he said, bobbing his head and smiling.

"Well, let's have one!" I wanted to say. Sensing my desire perhaps (as evidenced by the drool on my chin) his face suddenly clouded, although the smile remained, and he pointed to a cardboard thing hanging from his mirror.

I must have looked confused when he said, "Cookies!"

"Cookies?" I asked, knowing perfectly well that I was not looking at a cookie but, rather, what I could now see was a cardboard Christmas tree.

"Yes! Smells like cookies!" he said gleefully, as though the smell of freshly baked cookies alone should be enough.

Well, that was enough, alright. It was enough to drop his five-star rating to a no-star rating. What kind of nonsense is that? Make your car smell like a bakery and then tell your passengers that the only thing they'll be nibbling on is a cardboard Christmas tree? I don't think so!

So now we were down to zero stars — don't ever give me cardboard when you've promised me cookies!

But I knew Joshumel felt bad about disappointing me because then he began to chat. I'd already determined that English wasn't his first language, but that didn't phase him.

By the time we arrived at our destination I knew that Joshumel was from Eritrea (which I mistakenly pronounced Urethra), married with two kids and another on the way, is Muslim, loves America and basketball and hopes to one day attend college.

By the time he said, "You a very nice man," I'd already given him his five stars back, plus a generous tip.

Best of all, I didn't eat his cardboard Christmas tree.

I am getting very sleepy. Is this the gym?

Anybody who has known me for more than five minutes knows I struggle with my weight. How do they know this? Because I try to eat them!

Not really. It's because this bit of personal oversharing comes flowing off my tongue like everything that flows over it in the other direction.

Nobody is interested, I know that. That's because most Americans (over 2/3 to be exact) have their own struggles with weight. They are now described as "obese." Ouch. My dieting goal now is to always be at least one pound less than the designation of "obese." How's that for aiming high?

Still, I persist. Every time I try a new diet — and fail — I resolve to "never do another diet as long as I live." That's an easy resolution to keep, until somebody tells me they lost 14 pounds in a week of eating nothing but oatmeal and feather pillows.

But several months ago I decided I'd really had enough. "Brad," I said, "I'm going to have a gastric bypass."

He had his head buried in a book at the time and said,

"Oh? You're going to pass gas…?"

"No, I said I'm going to have a gastric bypass."

To his credit, he said he would support whatever I wanted to do, and when the time came he willingly accompanied me to the information session given by the local celebrity gastric bypass expert whose user-friendly name is Doctor Ronnie. This took place at a famous hospital not far from where we live and was attended by at least thirty other weight-challenged individuals.

The doctor was late, so his nurse did the presentation — just as you'd expect a flight attendant to fly the plane for a pilot who was caught in traffic.

Wait, what?

The audio-visual presentation was the high point, since it was a parade of formerly fat people who were now thin. I love that sort of thing, and it made me want to sign up on the spot. In fact, I didn't care if the doctor ever showed up — the nurse could do it! Let's get started!

But then the Doctor actually arrived on a cloud of self-importance and proceeded to tell us a bunch of stuff his malpractice insurance agent probably told him to say, all of which I've forgotten except this: *"Individual results may vary and these results are not guaranteed."*

Oh and then there was this: "Hair loss is *almost* always temporary."

And my favorite, "Gastric bypass surgery can help you lose weight, but if you don't follow the diet, exercise, and nutrition guidelines, you could gain the weight back after the procedure."

Okay, now let me be sure I've understood correctly: I pay you thirty-thousand dollars, my hair falls out, and if I eat less and exercise, I may get thin and stay that way?

We left before the question and answer period.

Then I had another idea.

I once saw the four hosts on NBC's *Today* show get hypnotized, and I remember that the hypnotist said hypnotism can be used for all kinds of things like stopping smoking…weight loss…and, well, that's when I stopped listening and ran to my computer to search for hypnotism guys.

A quick internet search led me to a "certified hypnotherapist" in downtown Palm Springs — a good 20 minutes from our house. "What if I'm still hypnotized afterwards and unable to drive?"

"Nobody will be able to tell," was Brad's smartass reply.

The truth is, I was worried about being "out of it" when somebody wasn't there to watch over me. I thought about asking Brad to accompany me, but then I wondered how he would keep from getting hypnotized just by being in the vicinity. On the drive downtown I began to fret.

What would I do, I wondered, if while I was "asleep," this charlatan decided to rob me? All he would need to do is go through my wallet, help himself to the cash and credit cards and put the wallet back in my pocket before he snapped me out of it.

I came up with a plan. I'd leave my wallet in the car. But then I realized all he would need to do is ask me, under hypnosis, if I had any money.

"Yes…," I'd say dreamily. "It's in my wallet in the car."

"Great. Be right back!" he'd say as I remained sleeping while he rifled through my car.

But a bigger concern was about the other stuff he would do to me....you know. How do I know this isn't just some pervert who gets his jollies molesting overweight old men?

Once again, I came up with a sure-fire idea. I would safety-pin my undershirt to my underpants so I would at least know if he'd tried!

It took me a minute but I realized that was equally ridiculous. What would keep him from unpinning my underwear and then re-pinning it before he brought be back? Another stupid idea.

I'd worked myself into quite a state by the time I got to his office, but either he had hypnotized me over the phone when I'd made the appointment or he just put me at ease by being a completely normal-acting person.

Somehow I knew I'd be safe.

It may surprise you that I didn't ask him to do anything about my eating habits. By now I had determined that my problem isn't so much over-eating as it is under-exercising. So, I reasoned, I will ask him to make me want to exercise more, which should have an impact on how much I want to eat — and how quickly the weight comes off.

He seemed to agree. "Okay, what do you think is a good exercise plan?" he asked.

"Every day," I replied. "Except one day a week when I will take it easy." This was be the exact opposite of my current plan which was to take it easy every day of the week except one when I would go to the gym and watch TV.

"Great. Let's get started."

But that's when things got strange. He didn't swing an old-fashioned pocket watch in front of my face and he didn't keep repeating, slowly, "You are getting very sleepy...." (Although I may be a good candidate for hypnotism since I almost put myself to sleep just typing that last sentence.)

Instead, he let me keep my eyes open and had me stare at a dot on the ceiling (a dead fly, I think) while he talked to me in a deep monotone. He told me to imagine going to the gym every morning...that I would awaken and immediately be eager to go to the gym... that I wouldn't do anything else until I'd gone to the gym...etc. etc. I don't know how long this went on — maybe thirty or forty minutes? But at the end he simply asked for his money and said he would see me next week!

I managed to find the car, and after I made sure my underwear was still pinned to my T-shirt and my wallet was still under the seat, I headed directly to...the gym!

It's true! It worked!

For several weeks — maybe three or four months — I went to the gym religiously every day. I knew it had to have something to do with the hypnotism because that would never have happened otherwise.

I only wish I'd been a bit more specific about what I should do when I get there.

This Place Puts the Din in Dining

We eat out frequently, it's true. As my friend Liz used to say, the thing she makes best for dinner is reservations. I strive to follow her example.

When we are traveling, we eat out practically every night. If we are staying in a hotel room equipped with a kitchen — something I strongly discourage — I will make breakfast, and sometimes lunch, but we always go out at night.

This month we are exploring the northern part of the state, using a little rental cottage in Sebastopol, California as our home base. From here we take little day-trips to the many towns and villages and maybe a winery or fifty nearby. Yesterday, for example, we drove about an hour and a half to spend the day with some friends we know from home.

"Bill and Polly" are a cute young couple who own a thriving business and, like us, decided to flee the desert heat for a little vacation. They rented a beautiful home with an unobstructed view of the ocean in Sea Ranch, a surreal community of a thousand or so homes located about one hundred miles north of San Francisco. The homes aren't all alike, but they conform to one architectural style and are spaced far apart on what appear to be one-acre lots. This is the community anybody would design if they had (a) good taste; (b) an ecological mindset; and (c) the ability to design a community.

When Bill and Polly first extended the invitation they asked us to spend the night, but we politely declined because we follow the old adage that "fish and friends stink after three days." True, they hadn't asked us to stay for three days, only one, but that still falls under *my* old adage that "a fish that stinks after three days already starts to smell bad after just one…."

But the truth is, we were just a couple of hours away from our own home-away-from home, so why wouldn't we just drive home at the end of our fun-filled day?

And so we did. We spent a lovely day together, walking, talking, exploring — and then we kissed them goodbye and headed home. I am proud to report that we got almost a mile down the road before we decided it was just too far to go. But instead of turning back and surprising our hosts as Brad suggested we do ("Hello! We decided not to leave after all!"), I insisted that we pull into the first motel we came to.

As luck would have it, the place we came to had only one room left, so we grabbed it. As we were registering, the desk clerk asked us if we needed reservations for dinner in their restaurant that night. "Do we need them?"

"Oh yes," she said. "We're fully booked!"

I decided not to ask her how we could make reservations if they were fully booked and instead asked for a table for two at 6:30. It was about 5 o'clock, which meant we still had time to squeeze in an Old Man Nap.

At 6:45 we managed to wake up and throw on some clothes before trotting over to the dining room — fifteen minutes late, which is unheard of in Rex and Brad World. "I'm so sorry!" I sputtered to the hostess, "Thank you for holding our table!" She eyed me suspiciously, no doubt wondering if I was being sarcastic. I hadn't yet noticed that the place was practically empty.

Then she smiled or grimaced, I'm not sure which, before showing us to the least desirable table in the place — right next to the kitchen. But I was still half-asleep and didn't feel like fighting. Besides, we were late; maybe this was the Punishment Table for people who didn't show up on time — a little two-top, far from the big windows overlooking the ocean, where one of us could feast his eyes on a wall of mirrors (guess who!?) while the other could sit surveying the empty room.

Apparently our server also expected us to be on time, which may explain why it took her at least twenty minutes to come by to see if we wanted a libation. Maybe she had done so earlier, at exactly 6:30. Finding the table empty, she must have decided she would ignore it (along with all the other empty tables) for the remainder of the night.

But she did come — eventually — about the same time three other parties were seated in the large room. We breathed a sigh of relief as we were beginning to wonder if the rest of the community knew something we didn't. At least now if we died of ptomaine poisoning, we wouldn't be alone.

About this time another server arrived too, so we knew things could only get better. This, by the way, is what is known as a false assumption.

After waiting another ten minutes for our drinks arrive, we began to hear a repeated shout.

It was only one word, delivered staccato-style, much as one might command a dog to "heel!" or "sit!" The command was loud, too, and we both jumped the first time we heard it, as though it had been shouted directly at us.

The problem was, we couldn't quite make out what we were hearing. At first we thought it was the word "Order!" — as a chef might shout to a server who needed to pick up an order that was ready.

But if that was it, the chef must have thought the server was locked in her car in the parking lot with the windows rolled up. That's the volume of the command we were hearing.

So when it was repeated several times in as many seconds — "Order!...order!...order!...order!" — we were left to wonder if (1) there was a courtroom nearby with the judge banging his gavel; or (2) if it was really coming from the kitchen, the food would start flying out frisbee-style; or (3) the chef was crazy.

Brad offered a fourth possibility, that the chef had Tourette's syndrome (which isn't funny but sad) causing him to shout some nonsensical word repeatedly. I said I doubted it because I think people suffering from Tourette's generally shout profanity. I know I do.

As we sat puzzling over this absurd one-word shout out, we made another observation. Every time we heard the mystery word shouted, a server would come around the corner from the kitchen into the dining room.

"Aha!" we said in unison. "They're shouting 'Corner!' — to let other servers know they are about to turn the corner from the kitchen into the dining room."

Now we understood, but we were no less annoyed. A minute later a third server came on duty and entered the fracas, adding a male voice to the two female voices we'd been hearing. Now we were sure: each server shouted the word "Corner!" every time they rounded the blind corner. This seemed like a logical thing to do until it dawned us that it could be done in a way that was less torturous to customers — especially those sitting next to the kitchen.

The dining room began to fill up, two more servers reported for duty, and this is when it got ridiculous. Now we had five people (seven if you count the busboys) shouting — I swear they were shouting — the word "Corner" every few seconds.

They might as well have been shouting "Incoming!" because I now noticed that we weren't the only people within earshot. Now all the diners seemed to jump or twitch or look anxiously toward the kitchen at each shout.

At one point I turned to look at the cute young couple seated about ten feet to our right just as they turned to look at us. We didn't say anything — we just burst out laughing at the absurdity of what we were hearing.

The next morning we had to return to that madhouse because there simply aren't a lot of breakfast places in Sea Ranch. Once again the dining room was mostly empty when we arrived but filled up quickly. I suggested to Brad that we both shout "Corner" as we entered, but he didn't see the humor.

Curiously, the morning shift of servers must not have gotten the memo or didn't care if they ran into each other, because we never heard the word "Corner" again.

We did hear a little kid announce at the top of his

lungs that he had to pee, though — so at least we knew our hearing hadn't been damaged from the night before.

"Corner!" I was tempted to shout back.

Surreal

I'm not sure I believe in omens, but when I looked out the window of our hotel room this afternoon, I saw a single seagull standing on the top of the flagpole directly in front of our balcony — about 20 feet away. He seemed to be staring at me like he knew me and was just trying to remember my name. I smiled at him, the way one does at strange birds, and he cocked his head like he wasn't sure what I thought was so funny. I made a face at him and he made one back at me.

I turned to tell Brad about this weird bird but he (Brad) said something else and I forgot all about him (the bird.) But we left our balcony door open, and I think that's where the problem started.

I know this sounds silly, but I think that bird was listening to our conversation. The reason I think that is because we talked about our dinner reservations later that evening at a seafood restaurant out on the pier, and I honestly believe the bird made a note of it — or whatever birds do to remember things in their little bird brains. I'll tell you why in a minute.

When it was time for dinner, we walked about three

blocks to the pier which took us right by "MOM" — the Museum of Monterey. We're both suckers for museums — particularly art museums — so we stopped to peer in the windows. (The museum itself was closed.)

MOM was featuring an exhibit of the works of Salvador Dali, one of my least favorite painters. I mentioned to Brad that my first awareness of Dali came in Paris more than twenty years ago — Dali was still alive at the time — when I visited his small "Espace Dali" in Montmartre.

Ironically, just a week before we arrived in Monterey I had read a piece in the *New York Times* about Dali's body being exhumed in order to obtain samples for a paternity lawsuit. Call me skeptical, but I sincerely doubt that the woman who was insisting on "Digging up Dali" (no, that's not a song) wasn't doing it because she forgot to tell him something; I'm betting that an inheritance was involved.

But as if digging him up weren't gruesome enough by itself, when they unearthed the body his iconic moustache was apparently still intact!

Brad's comment, appropriately enough, was, "That's surreal."

And this was *before* we reached the restaurant.

Since our hotel concierge had made quite a production about being able to secure a reservation for us (which earned her a nice tip), I wasn't surprised when we found ourselves being whisked upstairs to the "VIP section."

We were seated in a nice booth overlooking the water, and at sunset it must have been quite a view. I say "must have been" because they had roll-down sun-blocking blinds that would have enabled us to stare directly at the sun without incurring eye damage. I know that for a fact because that's exactly what I did. "Oh look — the moon!" I exclaimed.

"No, that's the sun," Brad replied, which only made me realize just how good those shades were.

In fact those shades made it look so overcast and gloomy outside — quite a contrast from the bright sunshine before we walked in — that I couldn't help but settle in as I would have in a remote mountain cabin in the midst of a Colorado winter — as opposed, say, to ten feet above the Pacific Ocean on a warm summer evening in Monterey. I ordered a Scotch and resolved to keep drinking until the imaginary snow storm passed.

As the sun dropped below the horizon Brad had the bright idea of asking the waiter to roll the shade up— and all of a sudden it was summer again.

And who do you think was sitting on the windowsill? (Hint: it wasn't the hotel concierge.) It was that same dumb bird — technically a seagull — who had the gall (sea gall?) to follow us to the restaurant! He obviously flew along overhead as we walked the three blocks to the restaurant and then waited until he could see where we'd been seated.

How do I know it was the same bird? Because of the way he stared at me. I stared back until a shiver went up my back as I realized that, for some unknown reason, this bird hated me. I had visions of Alfred Hitchcock's "The Birds" (we'd been in Bodega Bay a few weeks earlier, which was where the film was made.)

I guess I shouldn't have been surprised when that bird began to peck on the window. And by "peck" I mean he made a noise with his beak that sounded like a hammer.

Bang! he went and then cocked his head as if asking

whether I'd heard that.

I turned away to avoid his gaze.

Bang! He cocked his head again.

I was getting creeped out, and the woman in the booth behind me turned halfway around in her seat to look pointedly at me, as if to say, "What is it with you and that bird?"

Then Brad decided to play along and said, "Oh look, it's your friend."

I could have slapped him (Brad or the bird, take your pick). I hated it that Brad called him my friend. This bird already had an unnatural interest in me, so the last thing I wanted was for him to read Brad's lips through the glass and think that I considered him my "friend."

But that's exactly what happened, and he banged the window again.

By this time I was trying to quick-compute how much force that bird would have to use to break this gigantic picture window and, when he did, how I would escape before he pecked my eyes out. Note that I wasn't afraid of being sliced in two by falling plate glass —I was afraid of what would happen if that bird could get anywhere near me.

About this time the waiter reappeared with our complimentary "VIP appetizer" which was enough food to feed everybody in the restaurant. It came on something the size of a breadboard and was covered from side-to-side and end-to-end with assorted seafood. It barely fit on our table. The waiter said something about its being "courtesy of your hotel concierge," which is when I knew I'd tipped her too much. At this point, a standard party of two would have simply eaten the free appetizers and gone home.

We half-laughed when this monstrosity was placed before us and in doing so I happened to turn my head slightly and caught a glimpse of the bird on the ledge. He looked furious. I glanced at the tray to see if somehow we had been served seagull, but quickly determined that it was all fish. *Leave us alone,* I wanted to say. *It's stuff you eat all the time.* Then I realized that was what was bugging him. He wanted it. All of it.

Brad was pretty much oblivious at this point (his mouth was full of free shrimp) but I was miserable. That bird was still staring — and pounding on the window. But then my attention was diverted elsewhere: to the sound system.

The restaurant was playing, from start to finish, the entire soundtrack from The Wizard of Oz. Not just the music, but the dialogue as well. I assume the restaurant had the movie running at the bar and decided to pump the soundtrack through the speakers so all their patrons would know what it's like to watch a movie with no pictures.

Our entrees arrived a bit later and we ate them to the accompaniment of "We Are the Lollipop Kids," all the while with that damn seagull hammering out the beat on the window.

Surreal? You betcha. Salvador Dali's moustache must have been twitching.

Foreign Tongues

When I was filling out a frequent flier profile for Brad several years ago, the drop-down menu asked me to select between 'Mr., Ms., Rev., Dr., etc.' as an honorific. Without thinking too much about it, I checked "Dr." since that is technically correct for someone who has earned a Ph.D.

But to this day he is greeted as "Dr. Snyder" on that airline, and I shudder each time because I can't imagine what will happen when the guy in 28-C has a heart attack and they come running to fetch "Dr. Snyder" whose only choice, at that point, will be to teach him how to speak German. "Wie tut es Ihnen weh?" *How does it hurt?*

I was expressing concern about this one day when somebody informed me that they actually ask for "trained medical professionals" in an emergency. "Is there a doctor in the house?" is a line from a movie. They actually shout, "Is there a trained medical professional in the house?" which is quite a mouthful, but at least Brad is probably safe (along with the guy in 28-C.)

I am proud of Brad's many accomplishments, not the least of which is that he was once a college professor. When I slip this factoid into a conversation with new friends, they often break into German, as though he were suddenly standing before them in lederhosen, holding a beer stein.

"Ach, ein Freund, der Deutsch spricht, wie?" they'll rattle off, expecting a similar response. When he stares at them blankly — he's not a performing German monkey, after all — they seem disappointed. But English is his first language and like most people, he is most comfortable speaking in his native tongue.

Not me!

You don't have to ask me twice to speak in another language — whether I know it or not. That's because I have discovered, quite by accident, that you can fake a foreign language simply by listening carefully to the nuances of how it is spoken.

For example, everybody knows that to speak French, one need only speak English with a French lilt and sprinkle in an occasional "ooh la-la."

Ditto Italian — but you must wave your hands around while you talk and ask "Capisci?" after everything you say. But sometimes they simply don't "capisci" — even if you act out what you're trying to say. This is a lesson I learned in Cortina, Italy a few years ago.

I wanted to buy some Listerine, so I went to a half dozen pharmacies looking for that familiar green bottle with the cap specially designed not to come off without a hammer and chisel. In Cortina, pharmacies are like churches in the Bible belt or Starbucks in California — they're on every corner. In each pharmacy I would walk up to the proprietor and say, in English, "Do you have

Listerine?"

He or she would cock their head to the left or right (depending on whether they were left-headed or right-headed) and say, "Listerine? No capisci."

I would then hold my hand up to my mouth and blow onto my palm. Then I would smell my palm and make a vile face and hold my nose. In other words, my breath stinks! Or is it my palm? I could have blown directly into their nose, but I figured that might be overkill, so I acted it out instead. Is that so difficult?

Apparently, yes.

After I'd been to the fifth or sixth pharmacy I finally encountered a store clerk who spoke English. She hadn't heard of Listerine, but when I told her it was something you gargled when you had bad breath, she said, "Oh! you mean 'tooth water'! Over here we sell that as food — in a grocery store, not in a pharmacy!"

Listerine as food? And here I'd been spitting it out when I should have been swallowing it. Thanks, Italians!

Back to German. The German language is a bit different, because it uses what are euphemistically known as "gutteral sounds," which means you learn them in the gutter, while trying to cough up a hairball.

I only know a couple German phrases, despite the fact that I studied the language for an entire year in high school. I know how to say, "Ich habe einen grossen Hunger," which means "I have a great hunger." This is helpful, because most people are dying to know how hungry you are at any given moment, so I tell them.

I also know how to ask in German where stuff is. It's easy: simply to use the words "Vo ist," followed by whatever you are trying to find. For example, "Vo ist the toilet?" means, Where is the toilet. "Vo ist the

Cathedral?" will likely earn you the response, "Duh. See that spire?" But if you say "Vo ist the Berlin Wall?" you'll be told, "It's been torn down, Stupid. Where have you been?"

In the Czech Republic I discovered that all I need to do is add a "y" or "ie" or "zy" to the end of any word. For example, hamburger in Czech is "hamburgery." Toilet is "toilety." This is true! Look it up!

One night in Prague we ate at the "Crazy Cow Steakhouse" — which should have technically been called the "crazey cowzey steakhousy." The food was fine, but we sat across from two loud Irish guys whose brogue was so thick they couldn't even understand each other. Some "eejit" was being a "complete arse" and "bollocks" this and "bollocks" that — all at top volume and accompanied by great hilarity.

On our way home we saw that our landlord had thoughtfully put our garbage bins out for collection. This was our chance to see if we had been using them correctly, since they were clearly labeled "SMESNY" and "SKLO.".

I went up to Sklo and looked inside. It contained bottles and cans, so I deduced that Sklo must mean recycling, which meant Smesny must just be everyday trashy. Smesny, trashy. See how easy it is to learn Czech?

Don't be fooled — it's not just Americans who take short cuts with other languages and I have a great story to prove it.

When we were in Prague, we were delighted to discover a restaurant called The James Dean just a few blocks from where we were living. Yes, named after *that* James Dean — our very own "Rebel Without a Cause."

The James Dean turned out to be a perfect place for breakfast, since it was so close to our apartment. All we had to do was make it past a heavenly little Czech pastry shop emitting the smells of freshly baked bread and we were home free.

The first time we walked in the door we thought we were right back in the good old U.S.A. — circa 1950.

We were greeted by a striking thin blond girl whose upswept hair was partially hidden by a pale blue fry-cook hat, tipped at a jaunty angle. She was wearing a tight little electric pink uniform with a short shirt and low neckline. A white apron completed this ensemble. She was quite fetching standing in the middle of a the black and white tile floor with an authentic-looking American soda fountain in the background.

"Hello!" she said with a big smile. A second later she was joined by a clone: same blond upswept hair, same dress, same hat, same everything, including the same greeting. "Hello!" the second waitress echoed.

"Hello! Hello!" we said in return, grateful that they hadn't said "Ahoj!" which sounds a bit like "ahoy" but would have conveyed that they intended to converse in Czech, but this was before I realized all I had to do was put a "y" at the end of every word. But I was safe, since "Hello" obviously meant they spoke English, so we knew eating here would be a breeze.

We were shown to our booth which featured plastic-covered bench seats, a laminated table and squeeze bottles of ketchup and mustard.

"We're so happy you speak English," I said as we slid in the booth and they handed us each a menu.

"Hello!" they said in response while showing all their many teeth.

That was good enough for us. We ate there virtually every morning for the two weeks we spent in Prague. And every morning it was exactly the same routine: they greeted us with a big hello, showed us to "our" booth, and proceeded to carefully write down each menu item we pointed to.

We tried several times to further engage them: "Have you ever been to the United States?"

"Hello!"

"Do you have boyfriends?"

"Hello!"

"Is it possible to get the bacon extra crispy?"

"Hello!"

I wrote a postcard to one of my granddaughters and told them about "Missy" and "Sissy" (not their real names) and said, "They spoke perfect English — provided the subject was eggs and bacon."

Rock & Roll, Italian Style

Italians love their language and their culture, and why shouldn't they?

One day while Brad was out riding his bike I decided to take in some of that Italian culture at the local rock museum.

If you're thinking "rock museum" like the Rock & Roll Hall of Fame in Cleveland, you're making the exact mistake I made. It turns out that the Italian rock museum isn't celebrating Rock & Roll, it's celebrating… well, rocks.

What did I learn at the rock museum? Nothing much. Thanks to the unhelpful Italian-only labels, I ascertained only that rocks are divided into categories of big and small, old and older, pretty and boring. Most of them, I'm sorry to say, belong in the last category.

But I wasn't about to give up on Italian culture. The country is simply too beautiful and has too rich a history to judge it all by one rock museum.

So you can imagine how ecstatic I was to discover the "Little Church of San Martino," which is inexplicably located not in a place called "San Martino" but in the village of Fiera di Primiero.

This little church — and it is little, since it seats fewer than fifty people — is located on an idyllic hillside above the town where it has stood since 1206.

Yes, you read correctly. 1206, and I'm not talking about six minutes after noon. I'm talking about the *year* 1206.

This is where I should probably explain that I'm not very good at judging what's "old." For example, I think that 1906, the year of the San Francisco earthquake, was a really, really long time ago. True, it was in the 1900s, and since I was born in the 1900s, that would make me old — but not as old as the San Francisco earthquake, because there there aren't that many people alive today who were also alive during that earthquake (except for people over 112, that is.)

And 1206 certainly isn't to be confused with 1806, when Lewis and Clark came trudging back to St. Louis to signal completion of their famed expedition of the Louisiana Territory and the Pacific Northwest.

"Old" might be a hundred years earlier, in 1706 — 70 years before we became a country — when Benjamin Franklin was born.

But a hundred years before that, in 1606, ships set sail from England to establish a colony in what would be known as Virginia. And for most of us, that date would be pushing it for our collective familiarity with historical dates, but that was still 400 years *after* the Little Church of San Martino was built!

And 300 years after Christopher Columbus died.

And 100 years before Columbus died, in 1406, construction of the Forbidden City of Beijing began during the Ming Dynasty; and in 1306 the Mongols raided India.

And a hundred years before *that*, in 1206, Genghis Kahn got his start in a different part of the world — and the little church in which I stood that day laid its corner stone.

Why this little trip down memory lane — all 811 years of it? To make the point that this little church is really, really old!

And it shows. The interior features six windows and six wooden benches — benches similar to what you might find in a Slovenian high school locker room. At the front is a plain brick altar about the size of an air conditioner. But, believe me, it is *not* an air conditioner! The walls were once covered with murals, but today they are in poor condition, as most murals tend to fade every few hundred years.

The sign affixed to the exterior of the building notes that the interior of the church (i.e., the Slovenian locker room benches) had been "rearranged" in 1500.

By whom, I wondered. A pack of monkeys? Genghis Kahn? The benches are all helter-skelter and the floor has about...well, 800 years' worth of grime on it.

I don't know who their decorator was, but let's just say it wasn't Martha Stewart.

Forgive my saying so, but it's time for another rearranging!

Saving Lives, One Waffle at a Time

Most everybody knows about Eloise, the little girl who lived at The Plaza Hotel in New York City. She's the fictional kid who was always getting in trouble while terrorizing the employees and guests at the venerable old hotel.

Well, now the little imp has got some serious competition, right here on the West Coast, in the form of four ten or eleven year-old boys. I'll tell you about them in a minute.

Brad and I are staying in our version of The Plaza — the Marriott Residence Inn in Dana Point, California. Why, you ask? Simply because the cheapest room at The Plaza (as of this writing) is $760 per night. Cheapest room here at the Residence Inn: $127. Need I say more?

But other than the difference in rates (and the fact that the two hotels are 2,800 miles apart), the two properties are remarkably similar. For example, The Plaza is right across the street from Tiffany's on Fifth Avenue, while the Residence Inn is right across the street from Costco.

Ask Brad which he prefers.

It's true, we don't have bellhops and nannies and chambermaids to harass, as Eloise did, but we do have desk clerks and an occasional janitor type wandering around picking up the plastic cutlery and paper plates left over from breakfast. Yes, they eat on plastic around here. As I recall, they do not do that at The Plaza.

If you're familiar with Eloise's exploits (I remember she once locked a maid in a closet) you know she knew how to find trouble.

Now let me tell you about those four little boys. I don't know their names, so let's call them Alfalfa, Chubby, Froggy and Buckwheat — since those were the names of the original "Li'l Rascals," and, trust me, these four fit the description. The description should also include the fact that these Li'l Rascals don't know how to read.

They are, as far as I can tell, two sets of brothers, accompanied (at times) by two sets of parents. And, like Eloise, these four are "loosely supervised." But unlike Eloise, their kingdom isn't a 20-story building with 400 or so rooms. These boys are stuck on three floors with a little more than a 100 rooms. One of those rooms is ours. You can tell it because it has the "Do Not Disturb" sign on the door. That's how I found out they don't know how to read: *they knocked on our door and ran away!*

I answered the door, of course, only to find myself staring into an empty hallway. But I could hear sniggering, so I knew there were kids nearby. The noise appeared to be coming from one of the door insets a few doors away.

So I waited.

Eventually, they came charging out of their hiding place and ran down the hall laughing. I laughed too —

it's just the kind of dumbass thing I would have done at that age. Eloise would have laughed too — right after she pushed them down the stairs.

Curiously, these were the boys whose lives I had saved just an hour earlier. Was this their way of thanking me?

When I say "saved their lives" I may be exaggerating slightly.

The occasion was breakfast morning, the place where Brad's face always lights up and he whispers "Can you believe this is free?"

Well, yes. Look at it: plastic knives and forks, paper plates and runny eggs — in a *buffet*. Of course it's free! Who would pay for this?

I had just helped myself to a decent serving of watery scrambled eggs and a couple of pieces of burned sausage before returning to our table to read the only newspaper available: *USA Today*. ("It's free!")

Out of the corner of my eye I could see the four boys, who have been here all week. We speculated earlier that they are living here while their new house is being finished...or their furniture arrives from across the country...or Children's Services catches up with them.

Or maybe they just enjoy living in a hotel.

That was Brad's guess and I was ready for it. "For the yummy free breakfasts, no doubt."

We had already figured out a few things from conversations we overheard (the family volume control is set by the boys; you do the math.) The families hadn't known each other until they met at this very hotel and now they are all fast friends. After work the two dads sit and watch sports on TV; the two moms sit out by the pool talking endlessly and hoping the boys won't bother them.

On weekdays the kids are driven by one of the parents to a local school and the adults go to their respective jobs. We haven't been able to figure out what those jobs are except for one morning when I heard Mom #1 tell Mom #2 that she was off to "deliver a baby." From that I surmised that she is an OB/GYN or neonatal nurse. But Brad says she could be operating a black market selling babies and was simply going out to drop one off.

Oh, that Brad.

Breakfast is when we see them the most. The four boys have exactly the same breakfast every morning: waffles. The routine is always the same: they come running into the breakfast room and a few seconds later one or more of the parents arrive behind them. The waffles are prepared by the parents and served to the kids who sit together in a corner booth while the parents sit as far away as possible.

A few days ago there was a major problem when they arrived and discovered that the waffle irons were no longer located in their usual position atop a high counter. In fact, they were nowhere to be seen. This news sunk in just as the parents arrived.

Well. We rearranged our chairs so we could get a good view of the drama we knew was about to unfold. We weren't disappointed, either.

You would have thought these boys had been told their cell phones were being turned into mulch.

"No waffles!" one of them screamed at his mother. "Whyyyyyyyy?"

We couldn't figure out why the kid thought his mother would know the answer to that question. Clearly she didn't work in the Residence Inn Kitchen. How could she? She was busy delivering black-market babies.

But this mother was surrealistically calm. She looked at him as he was wailing like a four year-old and shrugged. Shrugged! This enraged the kid — and then his brother — and the histrionics were turned up a notch. Now they were both whining but at a higher volume so everybody in the breakfast room could enjoy the Vienna Sausage Boys Choir.

This went on — I kid you not — for at least five minutes before Marriott executives were summoned. The missing waffle irons were found, plugged in, and —- over time — things settled down. We moved our chairs back to their normal positions. Show over, folks. Move along.

But today there was a different problem. The waffle iron was right where it should be, and Alfalfa, Chubby, Froggy and Buckwheat were in their respective places, but the adults who made the waffles — the so-called "parents" — were nowhere to be seen. Uh oh.

We got ready to move our chairs into viewing position.

But after about ten seconds — when it became painfully obvious that these four had been abandoned and their parents, who had probably checked out by now, were twenty miles down Highway 5, Alfalfa decided to take things into his own hands. He would make the waffles.

This presented some logistical challenges. Alfalfa is the tallest of the four, but he clocks in at less than four feet tall. The fiery hot waffle iron, on the other hand, was conveniently located on a tall counter approximately five feet off the ground. On top of that, the iron itself — which was so hot you could feel the heat across the room — was designed to open upward.

As I computed the possible dangers in this setup I realized I was biting my lip.

Now, the mechanics of waffle-making are pretty much the same everywhere. Open lid, pour in batter, close lid and wait.

But this waffle iron included a new technology: spinning. The entire iron must to be rotated half-way through the cooking process. Presumably to allow the batter to bake evenly on both sides.

The problem is, the lid-opening and twirling are almost out of reach for a normal-sized adult — and certainly for a kid who is under four feet tall.

That wouldn't stop these imps, of course. Alfalfa had now been joined by Chubby, Froggy and Buckwheat and I began to wonder if they planned to stand on each others' shoulders like circus acrobats. But instead they simply stood on their tip-toes and tried to reach what was still clearly out-of-reach. I could see that Alfalfa, even when stretched out like Mr. Gumby, would only be able to touch the handle with the tip of his index finger at best.

"First degree burns," I thought as I moved to intervene.

"Need some help guys?" I asked in my best grandfatherly voice.

"Uh, yeah, you old dope," said Froggy. He didn't really say that, but his tone did. It was surprisingly sarcastic for someone who had just been saved from first degree burns by a kindly old grandfather-type who was now thinking of ways to accidentally put the kid's hand in the waffle iron.

But my good nature prevailed and I spent the next fifteen minutes turning out waffles like Kinko's spits out copies.

And let's not forget that I saved these kids from horrible, disfiguring waffle burns. Simply and modestly put, I saved their lives.

And what do they do to thank me? They play knock-n-run on my door!

Where is that Eloise when I need her?

Hello, Hell? I'd like to reserve some places for some people.

I like kitchen gadgets. I suppose that's strange for someone who doesn't cook, but maybe someday I will learn how to cook and then I'll be all set.

For example, I have a Spiralizer. That gadget, as everybody knows, is something you hook your cucumber or zucchini up to and then start cranking. At the other end comes out a long string of — well, zucchini or cucumber, or whatever you put in. (Isn't that always the case? You get out what you put in — sort of like life.)

The Spiralizer is an amazing appliance — even though it does require hand-cranking which is something the wagon-train people might not have minded, but I have higher standards. It should be electric or maybe gas-operated!

But, amazing as it is, I have used the Spiralizer only once and that was a long time ago. It is stored in one of the bottom cabinets in our kitchen — the ones I don't like to use because they require crawling on the floor and sticking my head into a dark place. Who knows what else is in there?

In addition to the Spiralizer I also have a little gadget that snips the tops off of strawberries. That may sound silly and lazy but it is incredibly useful when making a strawberry pie.

(You're wondering if I've ever made a strawberry pie, aren't you? Well, no. But if I ever do, I'll be all set.)

I won't list all the little gadgety things I have — it would take too long — but I will tell you about my latest addition: an avocado slicer and pitter. The truth is, I haven't used it yet and it currently resides in the Drawer of Stuff I'm Afraid Of. This is also the place where you will find our mandolin — which isn't a musical instrument, as you might expect, but a slicer that slices stuff so thin you can see through it. Have you ever seen through a potato? Well, I have! But it will also slice your fingertip off before you know what happened and who wants to see through a slice of their own finger? That's why it is kept in the Drawer of Stuff I'm Afraid Of.

Why am I afraid of the Avocado Slicer? Because it also tried to do me bodily harm.

Okay, that's not quite true. It wasn't the Avocado Slicer that tried to hurt me — it was the plastic packaging it came in.

Am I the only person in this country who thinks the packaging industry is out of control? I buy Gillette razor blades, and honestly, you need a razor blade to open it. And a box of band-aids.

Ditto the two gigantic Listerine bottles Brad brings home from Costco. Yes, my breath is minty-fresh all the time. Kiss me and see for yourself. Those two gallon-sized green bottles are more closely yolked together than two oxen hauling a cart full of rocks. I get out the screwdriver and pliers every time he brings two bottles home. It's either that, or I must hold one up above my head while I drink out of the other one — and that creates a weightlifting challenge of its own since they weigh approximately ten pounds each.

I want to know why they are yolked together in the first place. Is it because Costco is afraid some shoplifter will come in and slip one of those mega-bottles down his pants and take off? (You knew it would be Costco, didn't you? I mean really — gallon-sized bottles of mouthwash?)

It seems that everything we get is in some kind of hard-shell plastic container. I can understand if a product is inherently dangerous to leave exposed — like an AK-47, or something — but my multi-vitamin bottles do not need packaging that requires hedge trimmers to open. And neither does a surgical bandage. (Although with a surgical bandage, once you get it open you can use it to mop up the blood.)

Another example: not long ago we were staying at a hotel and I wanted to see what was at the bottom of the pool. (One never knows.) So I went to a local sporting goods store and bought some swim goggles. They were, of course, packaged in a huge clamshell made out of rigid plastic. I didn't think much about it and simply threw the box into my bag along with my towel, figuring I would open the package when I got to the pool.

Bad idea. Curiously, few hotels provide industrial-grade steel scissors next to the pool, so the only thing at my disposal was brute force. I began by trying to work my finger inbetween the two pieces of clamshell with a plan to just rip them apart. Ha. No such luck.

Finally I just threw them in the water, package and all,

and dove to the bottom to get them. I showed Brad how I could use them just by holding the package up to my face and looking through it.

Everything these days is wrapped in hard plastic. Why?

The small spotlights we use in our garden come four to a package in a clamshell that practically requires a chisel and hammer to open. The problem is that by the time you get finished with that hammer, all the lightbulbs are broken.

Enough, I said. I'm finished with the garden shears, and the pliers, screwdrivers and hammers. I decided to buy something that would make opening this crap easy. This turned out to be a "utility knife" which boasted a blade sharp enough to cut your shoes in half. The only problem? It was packaged in a plastic clamshell — just sitting in there, mocking me, daring me to get it out of its protective custody without cutting off my shoe. I refused to take it out of the store until somebody opened it for me. Curiously, that turned out to be an employee with — a utility knife! I resisted asking him how he got *his* knife out of the package.

Years ago, I occasionally watched a host on late night TV who went by the name David Letterman.

(That last paragraph was for the benefit on my younger readers who don't own a TV, much less watch it, and have never heard of David Letterman.)

Mr. Letterman used to employ various devices to elicit laughs such as "Stupid Human Pet Tricks" and so on. He went off the air before I could pitch my idea of a "Stupid Human Trick" — inviting the CEOs of two or three major companies to open their own products on-air. Ha ha ha! I can see it now: EMT crews being called and rushing on stage to perform emergency first-aid, possibly involving tourniquets and maybe a blood-transfusion.

It that ever happens, I'll bet those executives will go right back to their factories and change the packaging to something a child can open with her teeth or an old man could open without his.

(Yes, I have teeth. It's just an illustration!)

I've Traced My Family Tree to the Nuts that Fell From It

My cousins Donna and Linda have been part of my life for as long as I can remember. They were with me when our dear grandmother unwittingly sat us down on an ant pile for a picnic. They were also with me every time I threw a fit if I didn't get to sit in the front seat of the car with Grandmother — but they should thank me for that, because Grandmother's eyesight wasn't very good and it could be a terrifying ride at times. Those were the days before seat belts, so every time she approached a corner I prepared by closing my eyes and holding on to the door handle, but sweet little Donna and Linda got thrown from one side of the car to the other, bouncing around in the back seat like two lottery balls.

Donna and Linda also qualify as two of my "normal" relatives. (But don't let that go to your heads, girls — the standard obviously isn't that high.)

Growing up I used to look at the two of them and wonder how we could possibly be related. (I'll bet they wondered the same thing.) They were both blond with porcelain-pale skin whereas I was as freckled as a spotted owl. My friend Kathleen calls this a "disorganized tan." Age has now added insult to injury: most of those freckles have morphed into liver spots and the ones that didn't have folded themselves into various cracks and crevices where they await discovery by some unwitting medical professional searching for a vein.

Donna and Linda haven't changed much in all these years. They still look pretty much the same as they did when they were little girls — minus the sausage curls and crinoline skirts. How could I possibly be related to these lovely women?

The best evidence: all three of us laugh like we're demented. I only need to see them to start laughing. That would be rude if they weren't doing the same thing to me. Poor Grandmother. After one of our group visits I'll bet she needed a stiff drink.

In addition to Donna and Linda, I have thirty-five cousins on the other side of my family — give or take a few. When I look at that group, including myself, there is no question that we're related. In childhood photos where all the cousins are gathered around our grandparents' Christmas tree, we look like a rag-tag group of Irish orphans spawned by some ruddy-faced coal miner. Not a smile in the group — as though the photographer yelled "Your hamster just died!" instead of "Smile!" when he took the shot.

What a strange group we are. We may share certain physical similarities (let's just say I'm not the only one with freckles), but that's about as far as it goes. I don't think my cousins like me and for the most part the feeling is mutual. I probably shouldn't admit it, but I've wondered more than once if I might be adopted. Did I write "wondered"? I meant to write "wished."

For years I had a favorite aunt who tried to keep us all together — sort of. One year she even had the guts to put together a family reunion high in the Colorado Rockies. I think it happened only once, but the good news is there wasn't any bloodshed.

So, when Donna or Linda (I forget which) called one day to ask me if I would take a blood test, I was a little insulted. "You mean your side of the family doesn't want me either?" I wailed.

"No, you dope. We just want you to have a DNA test so we can learn more about our ancestors."

Oh sure. They were obviously angling to be written into my will. That alone is amusing since they both have more money than I'll ever have.

They talked until they'd convinced me that it might be fun to learn more about our Irish ancestors — or if we're related to anybody "famous."

"You mean, like Lizzie Borden?" I asked. Lizzie Borden, as you will recall from the song that immortalized her, "took an axe and gave her mother forty whacks…and when she saw what she had done, she gave her father forty-one."

"No, maybe somebody like George Washington," Cousin Linda offered, ever the optimist.

"Or Rin-Tin-Tin," Donna cracked.

Following their directions, I paid my money and waited for the kit to arrive so I could send a sample of my spit and see if it matched George Washington's. I could imagine some lab worker at the other end processing my sample and saying, "Hey, there's sawdust in this spit!" George Washington, you will recall, supposedly had wooden false teeth. So, if I were related to him, maybe there would be sawdust in…oh, never mind.

The results of my DNA were, to say the least, disappointing. It turns out that I am actually related to all thirty-five of my crazy cousins, or "those people," as I refer to them, and there wasn't anybody famous in the bunch. I am made up of the usual European stew of Irish, Scottish, Welsh and English — with a surprising dash of Italian thrown in for good measure (like oregano in the spaghetti sauce.)

Naturally I insisted that Brad take the test, too, not because I thought we might be related but because, of the two of us, he is considered the "smart one," and I wanted to find out if he had any smart ancestors like Einstein, Michelangelo or Stephen Hawking.

Ha! He wishes. But the problem is, we discovered that not only does he not have any smart relatives, it turns out he doesn't have any relatives at all.

"I know you don't have any brothers and sisters," I said to him one day as we were having breakfast, but you must have a cousin or two -- or 35, as I do."

"No," he stated. "Neither of my parents had brothers or sisters, so I don't have any cousins at all."

I sort of resented him at that point. Without cousins, who bullied him and made fun of him when he was growing up? Who broke his toys — or his nose? People *need* relatives, don't they?

So, I did the only thing I could think of: I gave him mine. (Donna and Linda, if you're reading this, come give Brad a big hug. He's your new cousin.)

Jerky

California is a big state. It is so big, in fact, that some people think it should be three states. These people are what we call "crazy," because that's never going to happen.

That hasn't stopped them from trying. (Don't ask me who "them" is because I don't know. All I know is that they're crazy.) But at one point these unidentified crazy people had amassed enough signatures to place the issue on the ballot in the next general election.

I do see their point, however. California is big — 163,700 square miles — only Alaska and Texas are bigger — and we are Number One in population: more than 37 million people. Some Texans like to brag that because of our high taxes, Californians are moving in droves to Texas, which has a population of roughly 25 million — and no state income tax. Well, that means at least 12 *million* of us would need to move to Texas before they're even close to being as populated as we are.

(By the way, population is sometimes referred to as "density" — as in, people who think they can divide California into three states are "dense.")

There are also fewer local governments in California: Texas has 722 more cities and towns than we do, but it should be noted that one of these "municipalities" is Guerra, TX located in Jim Hogg County, population: 6.

Yes, six.

Personally, I don't think you should be allowed to call some place a "town" if all the inhabitants can fit in a SmartCar.

We live in a small town too — a lovely little place called Rancho Mirage, California, where our "downtown" consists of a medium-sized shopping center. Rancho Mirage is located smack dab in the middle of the Coachella Valley, where one of the largest music festivals in the world takes place every spring.

We are a bit more than two hours from Los Angeles, but we have a population of only 17,000 people — which increases more than 15 percent during "high season" (e.g., what other people call "winter.")

But I'm not writing this during winter; I'm writing it in July when the temperature in Rancho Mirage averages 107 degrees.

In other words, I'm not writing this from home. Rather, I'm writing from an even smaller town than Rancho Mirage: Idyllwild, California — population 3,874. But it's not that far from home, and it took only a bit more than an hour to get here. There are big differences between Rancho Mirage and Idyllwild during the summer, notably that it's 20 degrees cooler here.

We are staying in what is euphemistically referred to as a "Cabin Court" which, thankfully, is not spelled "Kabin Kort." It comprises a dozen or so "outbuildings," not to be confused with "outhouses." These little buildings are arranged around a large central mud flat and collection of potholes that could sarcastically be called a "driveway."

(Don't ask me why I'm using so many quotation marks in this chapter. I really "don't know.")

Our particular cabin is located at the top of a slight ridge which looks down on a roaring stream. At least I assume it's a roaring stream. I can't actually see it, I can just hear it — which means it's either a roaring stream or a 12-lane highway.

The living room, dining room and kitchen in our cabin are all conveniently located in the same space. This eliminates the need for opening and closing doors. Similarly, the bathroom is located in the middle of the bedroom, so if you like putting on a show, whoever is in bed can watch you take a shower.

At first I mistook the refrigerator for an under-counter trash compactor, but when I went to put some trash in it I realized my mistake. Fortunately I didn't confuse the dishwasher with anything, because there isn't one. In its place there is a sink suitable for Barbie's Dream House which makes washing dishes somewhat of a challenge if you dishes are bigger than what Barbie and her "friend" Ken might use.

Ha, ha! You caught me. Nobody is washing dishes up here, believe me.

Today we ate lunch at a Mexican restaurant which featured a large patio. We enjoy alfresco dining (*al aire libre* in Spanish), but when we arrived it looked like it might rain so I asked the hostess if she thought it was safe to sit outdoors. "Oh sure," she said, seating us at a lovely table overlooking the parking lot. "You'll be fine."

By that she meant that we would be fine if we wouldn't mind getting drenched as we ate, because within five minutes we were in the midst of a torrential downpour. So we moved inside where from the window I could watch the basket of chips and salsa on our former table slowly turn into a basket of mush. The hostess eventually swam over and cleared the table and we were relieved that she didn't deliver the mush to our new table.

As we were walking back to the Cabin Court we spotted a mannequin at the side of the road holding a sign that simply said "JERKY."

To be funny I said, "She doesn't seem that jerky, since she's standing perfectly still." To prove my point I reached out to jiggle her when I discovered she wasn't a mannequin after all. She was a human being masquerading as a mannequin.

I jumped back, prompting Brad to say, "Now who's jerky!"

We've all seen those signs that young people twirl and twist and juggle at the side of highways. According to Wikipedia these are called "sign spinners," — not to be confused with human billboards or human directionals which are entirely different career tracks.

Typically, a sign spinner moves the sign (spins it, one assumes) in an attempt to catch the eyes of passersby. The Jerky girl must have been unclear on the concept, as she appeared to be sound asleep — until I got about six inches away from wiggling her.

It was hard not to muse about the sign itself as we walked by, since it wasn't advertising a cell phone service ("Cingular!" is common here) or tax preparation service — typically spun by someone dressed as Uncle Sam.

But "jerky," if memory serves, is a piece of cow leather that has been coated with rubber cement and baked as hard as a board — except you can usually pound a nail through a board and nobody has ever been able to pound a nail through jerky.

The one time I tried to eat a piece of jerky I thought it vaguely resembled a doggie chew toy and I almost broke a tooth when I tried to bite through it. I asked the person who had offered it to me (probably my dentist now that I think about it) how I was supposed to eat it.

"Just suck on it," he said, which I didn't find amusing until I realized he was serious. "Why would I suck on something that looks like a piece of tongue when I already have a real tongue in my mouth?" I asked.

"Because it tastes like bacon!" he replied. I was tempted to point out the obvious: that if I wanted to eat something that tasted like bacon, I'd probably just eat a piece of bacon.

But that would be jerky.

Strange Foreign Customs

A Muslim scholar in the 1300's wrote that "traveling leaves you speechless, then turns you into a storyteller."

That proved to be true for me when I decided to write a blog of our various adventures, beginning with our trip in 2009 when Brad rode his bicycle from Geneva to Nice (almost 700 miles) while I drove a rental car the same distance. That pedaling isn't easy, let me tell you! And by pedaling I mean pushing the gas pedal. I'm sure that pedaling a bicycle is a piece of cake.

Before our trip I sent an email to various friends and acquaintances inviting them to check out the blog as a way of following our travels. I told them I thought they might find it interesting, which of course it wasn't. Why would it be? We were the ones having all the fun "pedaling." They were probably just sitting at home guzzling wine.

But at least it took me off the hook from having to send post-cards.

On that particular trip I wrote about Brad losing a tooth — something nobody wants to do when you are 5,000 miles from home.

Here's what I wrote:

Brad lost a tooth tonight. A big gold one. Who knew he had gold teeth!? He told me after dinner that it was loose, and I cautioned him not to wiggle it and maybe it would last till we got home. This caused him to reach in and rip it right out of his mouth — without any pain, apparently. Or maybe he simply doesn't feel pain. But at that point we were both standing there with our mouths wide open — his from just having reached inside his mouth with his fist, mine from sheer shock.

He held the tooth up to me with a big (toothless) smile and looked so proud you would think he'd made it in art class. Honestly, it looked about the size of a ping-pong ball ("You had that big thing in your mouth?") and since it was gold, I exclaimed, "We're rich!"

He looked at me with that dry look he does and said, "Oh sure. I see a new car in your future. A SmartCar!"

"A SmartCar!" I said. "Well, if that's the case, let's pull out all your teeth and get a Lexus."

Several years later, in 2015, on a trip to Austria, Italy, the Czech Republic and Hungary, I tried to explain our motivation for writing travel blogs every time we took a trip:

For those of you who are new to our little blog, you should know that we aren't doing it for you (so there!) — we're doing it to compensate for our ever-failing ability to remember what we do from one moment to the next. At the end of the trip, assuming we don't develop blogger's cramp, we will have a full record of everything we did, which we will then have printed in book form.

We put those books on our shelves at home so we can resolve arguments about what we did on such-and-such a day. (We do this by taking the book and beating each other over the head with it.)

Ha ha. You can see that I was determined to be wry and amusing — or what passes for wry and amusing when you are in the middle of a 14-hour travel day, as we were on August 16, 2015:

As I write this, we are between planes. We left Palm Springs at 6 o'clock in the morning. The taxi picked us up at 4:30, driven by an over-caffeinated 25-year old who wanted to talk sports. At 4:30 a.m.! Yeah, like that's what we do in the morning:

Rex: "How 'bout them Broncos?"

Brad: "Zzzzzzzzz."

On the first flight, in the seat opposite me, directly across the 10-inch aisle, sat a vision in pink. Pink dress, pink sweater, pink belt, pink sneakers (yes, sneakers with a dress), pink socks, pink purse, and pink barrettes in her hair. She held on her lap a stuffed animal — at first I couldn't tell what it was — a bear? a rabbit? No, stupid me — it was an armadillo — and of course it was PINK. She didn't hold it as much as she clutched it — from the moment we took off till the moment we landed. She clutched it while she drank her soda. She clutched it while she read her book. She never put it down. For a moment I wondered if it was alive — a so-called "comfort animal." But I quickly disabused myself of that idea because (a) it never moved and (b) she didn't seem the least bit nervous and therefore why would she need a comfort animal? And let's not forget, it was PINK.

Usually if you have a fear of flying, you show signs of nervousness. Not this one. She was as cool as pink lemonade.

You're probably thinking I've been talking about a six year-old child, right? Wrong. This woman was 30 years old if she was a day, and although I only heard her speak once — to the flight attendant when she ordered her soda — she sounded quite sane, appearances notwithstanding.

The shocker was, after we landed and she gathered up her belongings, she shot down the aisle like I was chasing her — which I was — because she'd left her pink armadillo behind on her seat! Yes, the one she never put down once during our entire journey.

"Ma'am! Ma'am!" I called out. "I think you left your pink..um...your pink...um...." At that, she snatched it out of my hand, said "Thank you," and off she floated.

As you can see, our blog entries weren't exactly the stuff of which books are made. (And yet....)

Strange sightings on our trips are by no means confined to aircraft cabins. For example, on that same trip we discovered that Vienna was crawling with Qataris.

Qataris, as you probably know, are people from the nation of Qatar which sits right next door to the nation of Bahrain. I mention that little geographical reference because otherwise you wouldn't have a clue as to where it is, would you? Too bad you don't know where Bahrain is, either.

Qatar boasts the highest per capita income in the world which may explain why they also boast the highest number of spoiled brats.

We spent several nights in a hotel directly across the street from a big park. It was a lovely hotel, attractive and well-managed. Its only flaw was that at about midnight every night a dozen doors on our hallway would fly open and a bunch of Qataris would come spilling out, like clowns out of a clown car at the circus. They were laughing and talking at the top of their lungs and generally acting drunk — even though they supposedly don't touch alcohol.

After a few minutes they apparently instructed their kids to go up and down the hall and slam the doors shut with all their might. Slam! (Count to ten...) Slam! (Count to ten again...) Slam!

The first time this happened I complained to the desk manager the next morning. (I telephoned the front desk while it was happening, but I don't think they could hear me because of all the door-slamming.)

"Oh, I am so sorry," the very nice manager said in a clipped Austrian accent. "All the guests complain of the same thing — but there is nothing that can be done." And then he whispered, "Qataris...."

Puzzled, I said, "Guitars?" I guess he thought I was complaining about loud guitar playing.

"No, Sir," he said, still whispering. "*Qataris.*"

The way he said it I wondered if he had suddenly switched to German and was saying something about cockroaches or bedbugs — something that simply couldn't be talked about out loud.

But then he added, "They purchase most of the rooms in the hotel during the summer...," and at that he simply stopped talking to me and turned to talk to someone else. Evidently "Qataris" is always the last word.

Oh well. We might not be able to go to sleep, but at least now we know why.

Once we became aware of the Qataris, we began to notice them everywhere. One afternoon as we were standing on a street corner waiting for the walk light, we suddenly found ourselves surrounded by six or eight women dressed in full-length black burqas with small eye slits. I was thrilled — there's something quite exotic about seeing something so unusual up close.

As I was standing there staring, we were interrupted by a loud ticking noise which I immediately assumed was to allow the sight-impaired to know when to cross the street ("Follow that sound!") But Brad had a different idea and quickly moved to stand behind me.

"What are you doing?" I asked.

"I think she's ticking…," he said, gesturing toward one of the women.

"No, you dope," I whispered back, "that's a signal so blind people will know when to cross the street!"

Later, it occurred to me that he had stood *behind* me — placing me between him and what he assumed to be a bomb.

'Til death do us part, indeed.

Later, back in our room, it was time to do some laundry. I had already discovered that the hotel laundry charged 4 Euros (about $4.50 at the time) to launder just *one* pair of underpants. So since one of us is "thrifty," I decided it would be easier to simply wash out a pair of my briefs in the bathroom sink than to argue with Brad about how much it cost.

That was a good idea until it dawned on me that we didn't have a clothes dryer in our room — so how would they get dry? I considered hanging them out the window (and telling people it was the Qatari flag) but instead decided to wring them out really really well and then use the hairdryer to dry them the rest of the way.

This is when I made an interesting discovery. It turns out that fabric will actually *burn* if you get it hot enough — and I have the holy underwear to prove it!

I blame the Qataris.

Strange Foreign Customs Part II

"All journeys have secret destinations of which the traveler is unaware." -Martin Buber

I am ashamed to admit it, but I sometimes act like a tourist. When I travel to a place I've only read about, the first thing I do is hop on a tourist bus to get the lay of the land. The open air buses are best, because you learn to dodge bird excrement even as you enjoy the scenery.

But sometimes the bus isn't the best choice. In Sydney, Australia, for example, we were on the upper level of a bus that never stopped except at traffic lights. I wondered if we were being chased by the cops. We were going so fast we decided the pre-recorded commentary was being played at high-speed and the driver was simply trying to keep up. When we approached the Sydney Harbor Bridge and the iconic Opera House, the driver advised us to "be ready to snap some photos."

We were, but we would have needed a motion picture camera to do them justice, because apparently the reason he wanted us to be ready was that he had no intention of stopping — or even slowing down. When people realized the view was going to go flying by, we all moved quickly to the right-hand side of the bus and I expected the bus to tip over due to the shift in weight.

Later, on the same trip but this time in Wellington, New Zealand, we took a tour bus with a recorded commentary that wasn't even working (a fact they failed to mention when we purchased our tickets.) In this case, the driver wasn't moving or talking too fast — he wasn't talking at all. Apparently he wasn't about to be bothered to tell us in "real time" what we were seeing — so he simply drove us around in silence for an hour as we sat wondering what we were looking at. We became so bored we began making up things, which naturally we shared with the other passengers. "Oh, look — I think that's the only department store in the world that sells live kangaroos."

("Really?")

("No.")

We were so annoyed that long before the tour ended we jumped off the bus (no, not from the top level and not while it was moving) and ran all the way to the nearest pub.

On yet another tour bus — this one in Barcelona, Spain — I exchanged business cards with an important-looking businessman from Switzerland who was traveling with his teenage son. I still have the card, so the next time we're in Switzerland we can have hot chocolate and maybe go yodeling together.

"Hello, Dieter? Remember me from that time we rode the tour bus through the streets of Barcelona…?"

I must have thousands of business cards that I've collected over the years (minus thousands more that I've thrown away), and I'm not sure why I hold on to them. I've thought of leaving a note for my children telling them that when I die they should get in touch with all these people to deliver the bad news. That makes me smile, as I can almost hear the phone call:

"Hello, we're sorry to pass on the sad news that our father has passed away…."

"Oh, I'm so sorry. Now…um….who was your father again?"

"You spent 90 minutes with him on a bus in Barcelona twenty years ago. Now, do you think you'll be coming to the funeral…?"

I know it sounds maudlin, but then I imagine what it would be like if they all showed up. We're talking at least five thousand people and probably many more. If the kids charged five bucks admission, well, what a nice party they could throw!

Another touristy thing we do when we travel is Chu-Pa-Mu. That's our shorthand for churches, palaces and museums. We're both more Pa-Mu than Chu — but we'll visit the Chus because of the architecture. I defy you to walk into the Sistine Chapel at the Vatican or Saint-Chapelle in Paris and not gasp or simply say "Ah…" as you enter. That obviously makes those churches "ah-Chus." (God bless you!)

Here's a travel tip if you're flush with money and can't find enough places to buy 5-Euro cups of coffee: spring for a Museum Membership — even if you plan to visit only once. Typically it includes two free tickets and — best of all — early admission. If you plan to visit two days in a row, or 20 days in a row as you should when you visit the Louvre, that's even better. A membership allows you early admission before the hordes of tourists are let in. We spent a full thirty minutes completely alone in the Musée d'Orsay (my favorite Mu in the whole world) and it was awesome. It's a bit more costly than two admission tickets, but you can consider the extra cost as your gift to the local culture, which is a nice thing to do.

Or, if you're just cheap, you can go stand in line where you belong.

On a truly magnificent August day a few years ago we visited the Schönbrunn Palace in Vienna. We signed up for the Grand Tour — advertised as "40-rooms in 50-minutes," which is one of the worst marketing slogans I've ever heard. "This is simply an indoor jogging track," I told Brad.

And jog we did! But forty rooms sounds like a lot until you realize the joint has almost 1,500 in total. Fifteen hundred! I assume if you want a real workout you need to sign up for the "1,500 rooms in 24 hours" option.

The inside tour was followed by a tour of the gardens, which includes a maze. ("You've seen our house, now get lost!")

Over 3 million tourists visit the Palace each year and most of them, we discovered, like to come on sunny days in August. This is equally true of the Palace of Versailles outside Paris, where a stroll through the Hall of Mirrors as part of a big, thick mass of pulsating humanity (each with a cellphone camera and selfie stick) can make you want to jump out the nearest floor-to-ceiling French window, but of course this is impossible because the windows are at least twenty feet from where you are being propelled through the room — leaving you one of two options: falling to the floor and crawling toward the window on your hands and knees — and risk being trampled to death — or, politely asking in Chinese if your fellow tourists will pick you up and crowd-surf you to the window.

By the way, I wrote "in Chinese" in the paragraph above — not to be racist, but because we saw mostly Chinese people on our last trip to Paris. We rarely encountered a French citizen, and we often wondered aloud, "Who let the French out?"

They're probably all visiting the Schönbrunn Palace in Vienna.

After we exited the Schönbrunn, we headed for the subway which was — surprise! — quite crowded. When the train arrived (exactly on time, because this is Austria) I was nearest to the door, so naturally I reached for the touchpad to open it.

Nothing happened.

I pushed it again...and again — but the doors remained firmly shut.

Finally, a kind man reached around me and pushed a little red button just above the touchpad which actually operates the doors. I had been banging on a square of paint which, as it turns out, does absolutely nothing.

As the doors opened, Brad said *sotto voce*, "I guess this isn't the train for the gifted."

"I am not the same, having seen the moon shine on the other side of the world." – Mary Anne Radmacher

Bar Nuts

Many writers spend a lot of time trying to "get published." That's because unless you're writing a diary, you actually like the idea of people reading your stuff.

My writing career began in the 7th Grade when it was either that or mow the lawn. By that time I'd spent a few summers working for my dad's construction firm, and while I didn't yet know exactly what I wanted to do for a living, I knew that whatever it was, it wouldn't involve a lawn mower, hammer or shovel.

But just putting words on paper didn't provide much of a rush. I needed somebody to read what I'd written and give me a pat on the back or, if they were feeling especially gracious, the Pulitzer Prize for literature.

"I need to be published!" I cried. My grandmother heard my cries and found the perfect solution: a Hectograph.

A Hectograph is a thin metal tray — about a half-inch deep — filled with clear gelatin. After writing one's masterpiece on a purple "master," it is placed face down on the sticky gelatin for five or ten minutes, transferring your brilliance to the surface beneath. Then, one page at a time, a clean piece of paper is placed on top of the gelatin, smoothed out for a moment, then peeled off. Like magic, the previously white paper is now filled with the actual words you wrote only moments before! This is repeated as many times as needed until you have the number of copies you need to distribute to all the people on your block who, as it turns out, would rather have you mow their lawn.

Apparently I'm not the only person to launch his writing career on a Hectograph. In his book *On Writing*, my friend Stephen King who is a famous author and therefore not really my friend (yet), tells how he and his brother Dave used a Hectograph to create their neighborhood newspaper. But I wonder if Stephen knows that the Hectograph process is still in use today — not to produce Pulitzer prize-winning work but, rather, for temporary tattoos.

My next literary assignment was to write for my junior high school newspaper, *The Saints Roll Call.*

I attended Sinclair Junior High School and we were called the Sinclair Saints. By the time we got to high school we had become the "Pirates." The irony of moving from a Saint to a Pirate wasn't lost on anyone.

The truth is, I wasn't much of a writer and it didn't take long for our teacher, Donna Jo King, to assign me to "ad sales." All the boys thought Miss King was pert and pretty — which is what inspired me to make my first sales call on the beauty salon where my aunt got her hair done because it was actually named "Pert and Pretty." (Years later, a TV soap opera would be called "The Bold and The Beautiful." I like "Pert and Pretty" better, but who asked me.) I sold an ad, and then I went to where I got my own haircuts, aptly named "Sam

Hill's," because that was the barber's name. But after getting my first haircut there — an unfortunate buzz cut — I said, "What the Sam Hill...!"

I hated ad sales, so my interest in the school newspaper soon fizzled. My interest in writing wouldn't surface again until high school, when my English teacher made a big deal out of an essay I had written. I don't remember the essay, but I do remember the teacher reading it aloud to the class after which everybody applauded and for the next several days kids would pat me on the back and say, "Good job, Rex!"

Many dog owners say the same thing to their dogs, particularly if their dogs are named "Rex."

I thought I'd died and gone to heaven. I'd never done a good job on anything and I'd never had anybody pat me on the back unless they were hitting me up for a loan or a ride home from school.

All of a sudden that Pulitzer didn't seem so far-fetched.

Years later I would go on to jobs in which writing was an integral part of my day, and eventually I started my own public relations firm where writing was pretty much all I did.

It was during that time that my friend Teresa contacted me about writing a column for her very popular Houston magazine, *My Table*.

My Table was billed as "a critical guide to dining in Houston," and because of Teresa's amazing knowledge and expertise in all things food-related, it quickly became the go-to source for new restaurants, special dishes, industry news, etc.

Each new issue of *My Table* was gobbled up (speaking metaphorically; the magazine itself wasn't edible) to see which restaurants had been featured — because if Terry liked a place and said so, it would be booked solid for months.

I was surprised and delighted when Terry asked me to write a column about bars, saying she would like to showcase my talents.

It wasn't until years later that I realized she was referring to my ability to slam back three martinis and still walk home. Silly me, at the time I thought she meant my writing talents.

I said yes, of course — I would have said yes for any reason — because my "talents" were going to be seen by the world! (Or at least the gastronomical population of Houston.)

The Barhopper column premiered in June 1998, giving my take on new and old drinking holes in Houston — the ambiance, the bartenders, the drinks themselves. Best of all, I got to bill my drinks to Terry!

Recently I discovered a memo Terry wrote me at the time. "To Rex From Your Editor," it began. "You are so smart and funny! Your barhopper column struck just the right tone: half smart-ass, half-insiderish, half consumer reporter."

Clearly, Terry excelled in English and not math.

I wrote only a few columns before I knew I'd made a terrible mistake. I may have been able to bill Terry for my drinks, but I had a hunch she would draw the line at an extended stay at The Betty Ford Center.

A different magazine, in Colorado, sent me on "assignment" to write a column about a particular health spa in California. That was an immediate red flag, of course, because of the word "health." But when I found out that the usual charge for the week was $10,000, I decided it couldn't be all bad.

And it wasn't!

When my editor sent me a background package on the spa, I was surprised to learn that I wouldn't need to bring any clothes! No packing! Everything would be provided: warm-ups, T-shirts, kimono and sandals. When I arrived I was shown to my room which was notable for its simplicity. "Less is more," I was told.

The spa maintained a staff-to-guest ratio of 4:1 to "meet your every need without interruption or delay." Maid service was provided twice a day and included laundering of everything I wore. Now we're talking!

I also received a daily in-room massage which I especially enjoyed because I like rolling off the massage table directly onto a bed, instead of the floor as at a normal massage studio. Also included were two herbal wraps (which were not, as I discovered, something I could eat, like a ham and cheese wrap), a manicure and pedicure, an in-room breakfast, lunch, afternoon snack, and appetizers and dinner. Not only was alcohol not included — it wasn't available. For me, the former professional bar hopper, that was somewhat problematic but I decided I could deal with it.

The bugaboo, I decided, was going to be the food. The brochure had promised a "meal plan that reflects your dietary needs and preferences."

Well. Let's just say it was more reflective of the spa owners' idea of what my dietary needs were and certainly did not take into account my preferences. In other words, Doritos were not available.

When I made that discovery, I was offered something to console me: 12 hikes, up to 4 sessions with a personal trainer and over 40 fitness classes. I thought I'd died and gone to heaven! Did I say heaven? My mistake!

When I submitted the copy for my article after returning home, my editor looked up and said, dryly, "This must have been a very difficult assignment for you."

"No," I said, ignoring her sarcasm. "It was very pleasant and I would be happy to go again if you would like to do an annual follow-up."

Reading that story in my files now, years later, I realize I had been given an amazing opportunity: only 40 men were allowed at the spa during the week I attended, which was one of only four "men's weeks" offered throughout the year. My group included a movie star, a sitting U.S. Senator, the CEOs of two Fortune-500 countries and a man who owned 200 car dealerships. Several of them arrived in their own private jets and a few of the poor ones, like me, had to put up with being picked up at the airport in a Mercedes limousine.

After reading this chapter, Brad asked me if I would rather be writing about cocktails or spending time in a $10,000-per-week spa. I said, "It doesn't matter; as long as somebody is reading it and, preferably laughing aloud on occasion."

But I also wouldn't mind if I got to run around in a kimono all the time with a daily massage followed by a well-made martini.

Or to paraphrase the wry wit of Dorothy Parker*, I'd like to have a massage followed by a martini and I'd like to be a good writer. It's probably possible to have all three, and I hope I can, but if that's too adorable, I'd like mine with a twist.

*Ms. Parker's original words : "I'd like to have money.   And I'd like to be a good writer.   These two can come together, and I hope they will, but if that's too adorable, I'd rather have money."

Ink Blots

In the 2014 film, "Kingsman: The Secret Service," the main character, Harry Hart (played by Colin Firth), is heard to say, "A gentleman's name should appear in the newspaper only three times: When he's born, when he marries, and when he dies. And we are, first and foremost, gentlemen."

I wonder what that makes me, since my name has appeared in various newspapers almost as often as Jack the Ripper's — and I have the clippings to prove it. (To be fair to Jack, I am more of a case of "local boy makes good" as opposed to "serial killer on the loose.")

I realize that bragging that I am more famous than Jack the Ripper is quite a boast, and I can just hear my grandmother reproving me: "Oh, so you think you're better than Jack the Ripper, Rex? Braggarts don't go to heaven, you know!"

But surely I'm not the only person who gets a little thrill when he sees his name in print, am I?

However, I may have liked it a bit too much, as evidenced by a recent jaunt down memory lane in which I discovered that I have apparently saved literally every scrap of newspaper on which my name has appeared since the date of my birth until, well, today. *Every single clipping.* And I have the storage bins in the garage to prove it.

I say, do these clippings make me look insecure?

I recall distinctly how this ego trip began. I was in third grade, under the tutelage of my beloved Mrs. Mendenhall, who had arranged for me and my best friend Walter Parker to sing — *on stage!* — in front of all the parents and students in the school. I don't recall what the occasion was, but we were costumed like carnival barkers, wearing boaters (straw hats) and red and white vertically striped jackets and bow ties. We looked like we should be piloting a boat through the canals of Venice, but instead we were to do a tap dance routine as we sang a little ditty Mrs. Mendenhall had written for the occasion.

I don't recall what the occasion was, or the words to the ditty, or anything else about that performance, and I'm pretty sure I would have forgotten the performance altogether if it weren't for the newspaper clipping I recently discovered in a big box labeled *Memorabilia.* I assume my grandmother clipped and saved the piece from our little suburban newspaper, but she left off the date and page. I know it was from 1956, though, because that's when I was in third grade. More than sixty years ago!

That box of memorabilia is just one of half a dozen or so that I have been culling through now so my kids won't have to wade through it after I am, you know, *"gone."*

You can imagine my surprise when I opened the first box and discovered that it was full of trash — hundreds of pieces of ragged, wrinkled newspaper — looking like the kind of cosy container-bed you might prepare for a newborn puppy or litter of kittens. But upon closer examination I realized this trash was a chronicle of my *life*. Many of the pages were complete pages, ripped out in haste and stuffed away for "later."

At first I was puzzled. One entire front page of the *Rocky Mountain News* might feature the day's stories about a national crisis, a local crime and the weather. I'd be about to toss it in the trash when my eye caught a glimpse of my own name, referring to something I had said at a hospital board meeting. In the newspaper business this is known as a "teaser," and after you were sucked in you were expected to continue reading the article somewhere inside the paper.

I realized that it would take some time to sort through this mess— to retrieve the articles containing my name or photo and discard the rest. But it didn't take long to discover that the real news — the most interesting stuff — wasn't about me at all, but about what was going on in the real world while I was partying my way through Denver.

For example, in 1956 — the year I was prancing around dressed as a carnival barker on stage in my elementary school, Nikita Khrushchev gave a speech condemning former Soviet Leader Joseph Stalin, Prince Rainier of Monaco married American Grace Kelly, and Elvis Presley made his first television appearance on the Ed Sullivan Show, dressed in a red and white striped jacket, a bow tie and a straw hat...no wait, that was me.

Skipping ahead to 1981, I found a clipping in which my wife and I appeared in a photograph showing us shaking hands with First Lady Nancy Reagan. Mrs. Reagan was wearing a lovely silk blouse, my wife had on an expensive outfit I'd bought her a few weeks earlier and I was wearing a tuxedo. On the back of the same page I found an advertisement for a blouse similar to Nancy Reagan's on sale at K-Mart for $15.99.

So at least now we know where Nancy got her clothes!

I have now whittled down those boxes of — let's be honest — crap. I've trimmed the excess newsprint from the clippings but I saved them just the same, on the off chance that my kids might want to know that I once attended parties with people like Lucille Ball, Jessica Tandy, Hume Cronyn, Tommy Tune, Rue McClannahan, Debbie Reynolds, Mary Wickes, Angie Dickinson, Honi Coles, Juliet Prowse, Annette Benning, Marion Ross, Jean Stapleton, Daniel Travanti, Tim Curry, and Marie Osmond.

"Who *are* these people?" I can hear them asking as they sift through those clippings. "And what are we going to do with all this newspaper?"

"I know! Let's get a puppy!"

"The palest ink is better than the best memory." - Proverb

"Don't believe your own publicity. You can't; you'll start thinking that you're better than you are." - Leif Garrett

Fork, Spoon, Scalpel?

It's no secret that Brad and I enjoy dining out. Some people like to make lasagna; I like to make reservations.

My favorite Palm Springs restaurant is LeVallauris, located in an historical landmark building across the street from our popular art museum. The interior is filled with Flemish tapestries and Louis XV furniture, but we have never eaten indoors. We are always seated on the garden patio, surrounded by fresh flowers, enormous overhanging ficus trees and the scent of the clean desert air.

LeVallauris is "old school." By that, I mean the tables are set with crisp white linen table clothes and napkins, and a small bowl of fresh roses adorns each table. Each place setting is comprised of a Limoges china charger, crystal water and wine glasses and sterling silver flatware.

On a recent balmy day we were seated at our favorite table, watching the sun sift through the large canopy of leaves above us to create a shady collage on the table.

The maitre d' had just pushed my seat in when out of the corner of my eye I spotted local celebrity being seated a few tables away. We nodded politely in recognition, although he didn't have a clue as to who I am, but Brad was impressed because he assumed I knew him.

"How do you know *him?*" he whispered.

"What makes you think I know him?" I asked.

"Well, you looked at him and smiled…?"

"Oh, I do that with everybody," I said, smiling at the waiter to make my point.   He immediately rushed over to see what I wanted.

I briefly considered trying to keep this little bickering thing going — we do it to amuse ourselves, like those two old Muppet characters in the balcony — but it doesn't mean anything. Brad's always right and I know that, so I just like to argue with him to give us both something to do.

But now I was distracted by the menu chalkboard which had been brought to our table and set up on an easel, as if they were preparing to teach us a complicated math formula and needed visual aids.

It was the Prix Fixe menu for the day, neatly written out by hand in an elegant French-type script:

Appetizer
Soup of the Day
or
House Smoked Salmon Salad
or
Roasted Red Beet, Goat Cheese, Apple and Pistachio with Raspberry Dressing
or
Chicken Liver Pâté de Campagne
or
Butter Lettuce with Bleu d'auvergne and Walnuts

Main Course
Grilled Boeff Filet with Black Pepper and Cognac
Spinach and French fries
or
Grilled Fish of the day with Honey Lemon Green
Pepper Corn over Vegetable Medley
or
Organic Chicken Breast with Lemon Confit
Couscous and Rainbow Carrot

Dessert
Dark& White Chocolate Gateau, and/or a creamy,
Ivory Chantilly, Coconut Gelée,
Marigny Biscuit Chocolate sorbet
or
Trio of Home Made Sorbets
or
Grand Marnier Soufflee & Vanilla Sauce

The only reason I have included the menu (other than to re-live the experience) was to make the point that we weren't getting ready to eat a MacRib Deluxe with a large order of fries.

As we were making our selections, our martinis arrived (it was lunch, after all) along with the most decadently delicious French bread I've ever had this side of Paris — accompanied by a large pat of creamy butter with a fleur-de-lis stamped right into the butter. A small silver knife was placed neatly alongside each butter plate.

I was in heaven.

The astute reader will have noticed by now that there has been no mention of the way we were dressed. This isn't an oversight. The sad truth is, nobody dresses anymore.

I was wearing white jeans and a short-sleeved Tommy Bahama shirt. I had on boat shoes with no socks, and name-brand sunglasses shielded my eyes from the occasional ray that might make its way through the leaves above us.

Where we live, as with most of the country, I was suitably dressed for virtually anything: a night at the opera or a day on the polo field, going to church or going bowling. Coat and tie? You must be joking. Even morticians now wear luau shirts.

Seriously, in today's fashion, anything goes.

Except scrubs, obviously.

That's where I draw the line. Scrubs, as you are no doubt aware if you live or work in a hospital or watch TV, are typically a two-piece outfit made from thin cotton material with a deep V-neck and short sleeves. They are typically lime green or sky blue or plum red, depending on what your job is. The pants, notably, are held up with a drawstring which is cinched and tied in the front like a Christmas gift.

Sometimes — but not always — scrubs are worn with fluffy white shoe covers.

It was always my understanding that when scrubs are worn, a gauze surgical mask and cap should be worn as well — preferably in the presence of an open chest cavity about to receive a transplant. All of this has one purpose: to keep the hospital — and particularly the surgical suite — germ free. *Sterile.*

You can imagine our surprise, then, when into our elegant French dream strolls a man dressed head-to-toe in scrubs! He was missing only the paper booties, mask and hat. I expected him to walk with both arms bent upward at the elbows, hands in the air, as having just been scrubbed down with germicide.

I looked at our waiter, who was still standing by, and said, "What in the world…?"

Like all the servers at LeVallauris, he remained calm and totally nonchalant, just as he probably would if one of the large ficus trees had suddenly fallen on the next table killing all the diners.

He simply said, "Oh, that's a doctor."

Oh, really? I wanted to say aloud but didn't. *I had a hunch it wasn't a plumber.*

"Of course it's a doctor," I said politely but through gritted teeth. "I'm just wondering why…."

He inserted smoothly, "A plastic surgeon, I think."

"Oh. Well. That's better, I suppose." I used the back of my hand to gently smack the underside of my chin a couple of times. "At least if I need a few of these chins taken off after dessert, I'll be all set."

"Yes, Mr. John," he said, no doubt wondering if I was serious and he would need to get a sterile table cloth and boil some water.

I confess that I glanced at the doctor a few times during lunch, and when I noticed that he was cutting his steak with surgical precision I wondered if I might have been unfair in my criticism.

Hmmm, I thought. Perhaps the reason he's dressed in scrubs is because he's here to practice his knife skills.

All of a sudden the whole thing made perfect sense.

Of course I'd just finished my second martini.

•

At Least They Never Call Back

My former wife and I had been married for ten years or so when the phone rang one evening and the voice on the other end uttered those endearing words, "Guess who this is?"

Curiously, I knew exactly who it was even though I hadn't heard the voice for as long as we'd been married, but I felt feisty so I decided to play along.

"Harrison Ford!" I said. *Raiders of the Lost Ark* was the top-producing film of the year and had just won the Academy Award for best picture. Harrison Ford was hot, hot, hot.

My friend — let's call him Clark — sounded a bit miffed. "No…," he began before I cut him off.

"Alan Alda!" I exclaimed. M.A.S.H. had been on TV for nine years but was still enormously popular.

"No, Rex, it's…," but I cut him off again, thinking *you wanted to play "guess who," well, let's play!* "John McEnroe!" McEnroe had just won Wimbledon a few months earlier.

"NO, REX," he said, sounding a bit testy. "It's your old friend Clark!"

"Old?" That's putting it mildly. My old friend and

his now wife (I'd heard he'd married his long time girlfriend) had unceremoniously dropped us as friends after meeting a couple from Florida who seemed to take over their lives. Although we all had been living in the same city for the past ten years, my "old friend" had failed to return two or three calls, so I'd finally given up and moved on. But here he was again.

"Clark who?" I said disingenuously.

"Clark Smith, of course! C'mon, you surely haven't forgotten me!" (He sounded worried.) "You know... Clark and Linda...?"

I'd toyed with him enough. "Oh, *that* Clark! Sure I remember you, buddy, howzit going?"

Funny, but at that very moment I knew that he was up to something. I didn't know what, but I felt it in my bones. *Stranger-Danger!* as we used to say to our kids. My antennae were up and on full-alert.

"Everything's *great!*" he said, sounding like he'd just won the Publisher's Clearing House Sweepstakes. "But Linda and I want to get together to see how *you're* doing!"

"Oh, we're doing fine, Clark, thanks for asking." Then, softening slightly, I added, "Sure, it would be fun to see you again some time...."

"No!" he said. "Let's get together soon — tomorrow, even! Can we all have lunch?"

Hmmm. I don't hear from the guy for ten years and now he wants to get together the next day? I'm no dope. He wanted to sell me something!

"Okaaaay...." I said. "We might be able to get together tomorrow if you'll promise me one thing."

"Sure, Buddy, what's that?"

"That you won't try to sell me anything and that you

won't pitch any business idea to me."

Crickets.

"Clark? You there, Buddy?"

"Yeah."

"Is that okay? You promise? I think we could meet you at…."

"Why?"

"Why what?" I said.

"Why do you want me to promise that?"

Ah ha. So it was true.

"Well, Clark, it's like this. You haven't called us for ten years and then you call and pretend like we're long lost friends. But I sense that it's not because you want to be friends again so much as that you want to sell me something or pitch something to me…and I'm just telling you right now if that's the reason, I'm not interested."

"Fine, then have a great day." Click.

And that was that. I'd say my feelings were hurt, but they really weren't. I felt like I'd dodged a bullet — something I don't normally do because I'm as gullible as the next person.

Case in point: years later, after I was divorced and living in Houston, I was sitting on the patio of a coffee shop with a latte when a drab looking woman holding a baby in her arms approached my table.

"Excuse me, Sir," she began. "I am very sorry to disturb you, but my car broke down just down the street here and I don't have my cell phone. May I use yours to call my husband?"

"Sure," I said, "have a seat." And I handed her my cell phone. I don't remember the conversation word-for-word, but it went something like this:

"Hey hon. You won't believe the day I'm having. I wish you weren't out of town! First of all, my purse got stolen with all the money you left us for the rest of the week...." (Pause, while she "listens" to her husband's reply.)

"I know, I know. I know I shoulda...what? Yes, (she shakes the baby at this point) his cough is a little better but I'm on the way to the doctor right now to pick up some new medicine...." (Another pause to listen.)

"I *know*, Rob Roy [I doubt that was his name] but I can't help it! And now..." (tears appear as if by magic) "...the car just broke down and I don't know what to do!"

At this, she pushes "disconnect" on my phone and turns and sobs into her baby as she stands and prepares to leave.

At this point any intelligent person would have applauded and offered to nominate her for an Academy Award, but not me. Instead, I patted her on the shoulder and said, "Now, now" or something equally inane before I said, "Maybe I can help you...."

She looked up hopefully. "Really? You'd do that for a complete stranger?"

"Sure," I said. "First let's go look at that car..."

"Oh no! That's not necessary," she said, "I was able to park it safely to the side of the road and I'll make Rob Roy deal with it when he gets back in town. Right now I just need to take a taxi to the doctor's office and get the new medicine he's promised...."

"Well, do you need some money?" I was already reaching for my wallet.

She told me she was fine except she might need taxi fare to the doctor and then back home afterward. She said her sister would probably loan her funds to make it till her husband got home and that she would pay me back the next day, in the same spot where we were sitting.

After some discussion it was agreed that $50 would get her to the doctor and back home again. Fortunately, I had just come from the bank and had about $100 in my wallet. I asked her if she needed more, but she refused and promised she would meet me there, at the same table, at the same time the next day because her sister would loan her the money to pay me back my fifty dollars until Rob Roy got home.

Guess who never saw her again?

If you guessed me, you guessed wrong, because I did see her again — but it was about two *months* later — on the patio of the same restaurant. She came right up to the man sitting at the table next to mine and said, "Excuse me Sir, I'm very sorry to disturb you, but my car broke down and…."

At this, I turned around in my seat and addressed the guy, "Don't fall for it, Buddy — she did the same thing to me a couple of months ago…." Then, looking at her while I continued to address him, I added, "And it cost me fifty bucks that she still owes me."

By this time she was on her way out of the restaurant. "I've never seen you in my life!" she hissed over her shoulder. "And I sure as hell don't owe you any money!"

As we watched her dash across the parking lot and jump into a car driven by some guy — Rob Roy, maybe? — I said, "Well, that was a lesson I won't forget. What can I say? I'm an idiot!"

The guy said, "No you're not. She pulled the same

stunt on me, too, a month or so ago at this same table. But I only gave her twenty bucks!"

Tightwad I thought, before deciding it was better to be a tightwad than a dope like me.

Nobody wants to be taken advantage of and I suspect that many people who have generous hearts learn to be cautious if not downright suspicious the first time they are victims of a scam.

My late stepmother had no time for people who called to tell her she'd won something or had a deal that was just too good to pass up. She kept a wooden duck whistle next to her phone that, when blown, sounded like a whole flock of ducks quacking at full volume. When a phone solicitor called, instead of politely saying, "No thank you," she would blow that whistle with all her might right into the phone receiver. Then she would laugh maniacally before hanging up.

The first time I witnessed this performance I was aghast. "What on earth, Mother!" I said. "Why would you do such a thing?"

Her answer was short and sweet: "Because then they never call back."

Dress Code

We were having dinner at a sweet little restaurant in the beach city of San Clemente, California when a middle-aged couple walked in and were seated directly across from us. Notice I didn't say they "took seats," I said they were "seated." In other words, this place had a maitre d' at the door, not peanut shells on the floor.

I think it's tacky and rude to make judgments about people based on the way they're dressed, but I'd be a liar if I didn't admit that I sometimes do it — and I'll bet you do, too:

- That woman in her pajamas at the Mini-Mart? ("I wonder if she's sleep-walking?")
- The guy wearing cargo shorts at a formal wedding. ("Maybe he needs the pockets for the rice he plans to throw afterward…")
- The portly man wearing a thong bikini at the beach? ("No. Just no.")

See, it's not very nice, but we all do it occasionally — and this night was one of those occasions.

It was hard not to notice that this couple "stood out," even in a town where casual attire is the norm. In San Clemente, it's not at all uncommon to pass shirtless men on the street, or a barefoot couple walking their dog. This is all perfectly understandable, because the beach is at the bottom of the hill and who dresses up for the beach, right?

But we weren't at the beach. We were in a nice (and highly recommended) restaurant. One of a handful of "upscale" joints within walking distance of the condo we'd rented for a few weeks.

It was our first visit to this particular restaurant and we were looking forward to a nice quiet evening with good food in nice surroundings. This place checked off all the boxes we look for: clean, well-lighted (but not too light since bright lights tend to bring out my wrinkles), linen table cloths and napkins — and, most important, quiet enough that we are able to hold a conversation without cupping our hands around our mouths. Check, check, check and check!

But this couple looked like they might have a different check list in mind. Frankly, when they were seated I wondered if they wouldn't decide it wasn't what *they* wanted; that perhaps they would rather look for a local food truck instead. But they stayed, so I thought, "Good for them!"

Before you start making judgments about me making judgments, let me just say that it didn't bother me at all that they looked "unkempt." True, the guy didn't look like me (I have deep wrinkles that show up in light, but not a beard that would have made Grizzly Adams jealous.) But I don't expect everybody to look like me, nor do I want them to.

Besides, if they could afford this place, who the hell was I to criticize the way they looked? Were they over there saying, "Look at that portly guy shoveling those mashed potatoes in his mouth"?

(This is a distinct possibility — and they would have had every right to do so, since that's exactly what I was doing. And I'll just tell you right now, those were the best mashed potatoes I've ever eaten.)

So I was prepared to ignore them for the rest of the evening, silently wishing them a pleasant meal and good health and happiness.

But.

I couldn't seem to move past the fact that this guy broke one of my cardinal rules: he was wearing a hat.

Full disclosure: I don't wear hats. Ever. My head is oversized — about the size of a basketball by most estimates — and there isn't a hat on the planet that looks good on me.

But that doesn't mean I am predisposed to dislike people who wear hats. Au contraire! My son and son-in-law both wear baseball caps around-the-clock (or so it seems) whenever I am around them, and they look great. One is a Yankees hat and the other says U.K. which I thought stood for United Kingdom until son-in-law corrected me.

So it's not just hats — it's hats worn indoors -- and both son and son-in-law know enough to take them off indoors.

I don't know why that bothers me so much, but it does. In the "olden days" as my grandfather might say, a gentleman, whether he was a ditch digger, farmer, banker or bank robber, knew enough to take his hat off inside a building. Why on earth would you leave it on?

It's not stapled to your head, is it? It won't rain indoors, will it? That's a lamp on your table, not the sun, so you probably won't need to shade your eyes. So why leave it on? If your head is prone to coldness, put a napkin on your head, but *take that hat off*.

Naturally, this prompted a discussion between Brad and me.

The rules with which we were both raised (elbows off the table, please and thank you, don't talk with your mouth full, etc.) were pretty much the same for both of us, so it wasn't necessary to debate the hat thing. Hats are to be worn outdoors, period.

What we talked about is why it matters.

Why should we care — or even notice — what somebody wears? What's it to us? Does it change the taste of our food? No. Does it affect the speed or courtesy of the server? No. Then why, oh why, does it bother me so much?

The conversation took an odd turn when I tried to sift my hat prejudices through my current political philosophy.

As most of my friends know by now, I spent the majority of my adult life as a strong conservative, politically speaking. Conservatives and liberals are alike in that both make all kinds of judgments about how and why people should behave a certain way.

We make those judgements because that's what we've been taught, and to be fair, I think we *all* want to live in a civilized society — conservatives and liberals alike. The only disconnect comes when we try to define what that means, that is what is acceptable and what is not. For most of us, everything would be just fine if everybody would simply look and act like *us*.

I sneaked another glance at the man across the restaurant and felt ashamed of myself.

Brad was only too happy to help me sort out my thinking. "Look at it this way," he said, "a dress code is just a social construct." (Yes, he talks like that.)

"A what?" I asked.

"A social construct. You could bring fifty people into this restaurant, all naked, and you wouldn't be able to tell much about them…"

"Want to bet?"

He ignored me and went on. "But when they come in fully clothed, we can make all sorts of assumptions about them — the kind of work they do, how much money they have, what their educational background is, and so forth. But we could be wrong. What if the clothes they were wearing weren't the clothes they usually wear? What if they were borrowed….?"

"Borrowed clothes?" I said. "Who borrows clothes?"

"But if that happened," he said, pressing on, "the judgments we make could be wrong…."

I interrupted again. "You mean sort of like Cinderella after her fairy godmother got done with her…or The Prince and the Pauper…."

"Well, okay…."

Now I just wanted to mess with Brad, to tease him.

"Wait. You never explained why we brought fifty naked people into this restaurant to begin with."

He sighed and we moved on to another topic. But the more I thought about it, the more I liked that idea of filling a restaurant with fifty naked people.

At least they wouldn't be wearing hats indoors.

My Pen Pals

Attention, readers! Do you know Mizue Aoki?

How about Daniel Vanlangenaker?

Elisabeth Bayer?

Yes, those are names of real people, and the reason I ask is, I owe each of them a letter and I don't know where to send it.

The letter I need to send would go something like this:

Dear Pen Pals,

Remember that letter you sent me back in 1965?

Yes, I realize it's been over 50 years, but I hope you'll understand that I've been a bit busy. I graduated from high school, went to college, got married, had two kids, got divorced, came out of the closet, did reasonably well in business, published a few books and did some traveling.

And you? What's new? How are things in [Kleefeld, Germany; Brussels, Belgium; Kanagawa, Japan]?

Do you still love the Beatles, Elisabeth?

Is Natalie Wood still your favorite movie star, Mizue?

If so, I'm afraid I have some bad news for you.

And Daniel, are you still jujitsu-ing? How are your sisters Georgia, Denise and Liliane? If I'm not mistaken they're in their 60s, 70s, and 80s by now. My, how time flies! By the way, I'm sorry I couldn't comply with your request to write my letters in French or German. Surely you've heard that most Americans cannot speak a foreign language. Well, they can't write or read foreign languages, either. But you should be pleased to know that I at least made an effort. In fact, I have taken countless French and German classes over the years so I could correspond with you, but pretty much all I can do is ask where the bathroom is and order a cup of coffee — and not necessarily in that order.

The world has certainly changed since we were sending letters back and forth, hasn't it? For example, thanks to Google Streetview I was able to see where each of you lived back then — except you, Mizue. Google maps wasn't able to find your address in Tokyo — or if it did, I couldn't tell because most of the street names are in Japanese, and French and German aren't the only languages I can't read, write or speak!

Are you surprised that I have saved all your letters all these years? I am! I once lost my own passport in my own house — but I have somehow managed to not only keep your letters, but haul them around with me every time I moved. They were with me in Colorado, then Houston, then back to Denver, and now in California. Not only that, but I kept my own letters to you, which was no easy trick since we were all growing up before the days of photocopiers and scanners. Back then, I actually made carbon copies of my letters to each of you so I wouldn't repeat myself the next time I wrote.

How do you say "anal-retentive" in German/French/ Japanese?

I will admit that in all those years of keeping your letters so close to my heart or, more accurately, in a plastic bin in my garage — I have never bothered to read them, or my replies to you, since I first received them.

But I did today, and it was like hearing from you for the first time again!

Liz, I'm so glad that Berlin Wall came tumbling down, aren't you? It had been in place only for four years when you and I first began exchanging letters, and yet neither one of us mentioned it. The closest we came was when I wrote that I wished "Russia and China and Germany and everyone could be friends." I still wish that, but other than the fall of the Berlin Wall, not much has changed. But at least you'll be happy to know that I no longer spout such pablum; now I am consumed by American politics and let's just say I know better than to make such a wish.

Oh, and it turns out that my plans to "be a doctor" changed somewhat when I realized that math and science might be involved. Hope you're not too disappointed. I did enjoy seeing that plan, written in my own handwriting, since I don't recall thinking for a second that I could ever become a doctor! Hmmm…do you suppose I was just trying to impress you?

Mizue, I'm not sure I ever answered your question about "Spring clothes." You asked if I bought them and if they were blue or yellow. The answer to your question then, as now, is yes, I buy clothes in the Spring, but also in all the other seasons even though the only season we have in Southern California is Summer. And yes, most of my clothes are blue, but not yellow! (Really? Yellow?) But I am more concerned with fit than color these days.

And as far as your question about the "chopsticky," first, thank you again for sending them and yes, I was able to master them finally — with a great deal of practice. I actually think I may have lost a few pounds during the learning period as I dropped as much food in my lap as made it into my mouth. No wonder Japanese people are so thin!

Daniel, I hardly know what to say about the stack of letters I have from you, because I can't read a word of them! I vaguely recall asking my German teacher in high school (shout-out to Herr Belke!) if he would translate one, and he took one look at it and suggested I ask Mademoiselle Curtis since it was written in French. Who knew they speak French in Belgium!

That should tell you everything you need to know about my ability to learn foreign languages.

But somebody must have translated them at some point because I made a note in the margin that says, "Likes Peter, Paul and Mary." Well, Dan, I hope your musical tastes have expanded over the years because "Puff the Magic Dragon" wore thin after we all heard it a few million times.

I must say I am a bit surprised that none of you seems to have made it to Facebook. I did a search for all three of you and actually found three Mizues, and a couple of Elisabeth Bayers — but if you follow American custom (but why would you?) it is possible that you two girls may now have different married names. Based on the Facebook photos of these people with your exact names, you appear to be the same age as when we were exchanging letters and photos — which is highly unlikely, so I'm guessing those people are true doppelgangers. Yes, "doppelganger" is a real English word, although I am the only person who has used it since the 1930s.

But you, Daniel, should still be around, and unless you are living in Belgium's Witness Protection Program, you are probably still using your original name — so why aren't you on Facebook? I was a bit surprised to see how common the name Vanlangenacker is in Belgium. It's sort of like "Smith" or "Jones" in the United States, isn't it? But I hope you'll admit that Vanlangenacker doesn't exactly slide off the tongue, does it? Have you considered Smith or Jones? Just kidding! It's a great name and it's fun to say. It reminds me of another fun name to say: Englebert Humperdinck — who, as you may recall, was a famous pop singer back when you were stuck on Peter, Paul and Mary. (Incidentally, PP&M had six million-selling gold singles during their careers, which is impressive until you realize that Englebert Humperdinck has sold 150 million records in his lifetime! Most of those songs are still being played — repeatedly — in our "ascenseurs" and if they are, let's just say it's a long ride from the lobby to the 34th floor of any building where they have "Mandy" on a loop!

By the way, I did send Facebook messages to all of you — or whoever those other people are who are walking around with your names — hoping that maybe one of them is a relative who can tell me where you now live. But so far I haven't heard anything back. If I do, it will no doubt be from one of your kids or grandkids. I just hope they won't tell me you're out standing by the mailbox awaiting that letter I owe you.

Our Non-Trip to Slovenia

Have you, dear reader, ever been to Slovenia? Me, neither. Have you even heard of it? Me, neither. But a few years ago I almost went there and actually got within twenty feet of it. Does that count?

I'll tell you all about it, but first some background…

Like most of our trips, this one began at four o'clock in the morning. Our plane didn't leave until six o'clock, but we do what old men do — we show up early. Very early.

So at exactly four o'clock, our pre-ordered taxi showed up in our driveway where we were standing in the dark like poor lost souls — with seven pieces of luggage.

The taxi was being driven by a kid who looked to be about eighteen years old, complete with acne and an attitude. I saw him blink and then squint when he saw our suitcase line-up.

"Um…are all those going?" he asked with a slight tremor in his voice.

No, I wanted to say, we just keep our bags out in the driveway for convenience — you know, so if we ever need to go somewhere in a hurry, we'll be ready.

But instead I cheerfully responded, "Yes, we're going to be away for a few months, and you know, you need a lot of clothes for a long trip…," but I felt his judgment and I knew we deserved it.

In fact, only a year earlier we were in Europe and held quite a discussion on a train platform about what idiots we were to bring so much luggage. "We need to learn to pack more wisely," I said.

Brad agreed, so instead of the six pieces we were traveling with back then, now we have seven. At this rate we should probably look into leasing a steam ship.

But Taxi Boy just shrugged and started piling the bags in.

Our first stop was in Dallas, where we changed planes. (Yes, we'll get to Slovenia. Be patient.) We were also hungry, so we stopped at the first place we came to in the airport. We managed to find an establishment that featured sticky, icky tables so naturally we sat down to be served. After several minutes it became obvious that wasn't going to happen, so I walked up to the bartender and said, "Are we supposed to order our meals here?"

He said, "We don't serve lunch until 11 o'clock."

Since it was 11:08, all I had to do was arch my eyebrows and look at my wrist (that's where I wear my imaginary watch) to jar him into action. We ended up eating nondescript hamburgers and my arm kept sticking to the table, so I doubt we'll go back.

Next stop: London…then Vienna…and finally Slovenia!

After we'd been in Austria for a few weeks, the entire sound track to "The Sound of Music" was on a twenty-four hour loop in my head. Or maybe, just maybe, they were playing it from loud speakers on the streets and I just thought it was in my head. Regardless, as Maria once endearingly taught us, "Let's start at the very beginning…."

On second thought, let's not. Let's start at the very end.

I did not go to Slovenia.

I wanted to — oh God, I wanted to! But we never made it. Here's the story.

First, our rental car. We were in Vienna for several days before the bicycling portion of our trip was to start, so we didn't need a car. We took public transportation and the occasional Uber, but mostly we just walked.

But on the day before the cyclists were due to begin the journey over the Alps to Italy, we walked to the Hertz office to pick up our rental car.

I don't know what I expected, but this wasn't it. It was a Citroen model which we never see in the United States, probably because it's made in France and as far as I know is the only design mistake the French ever made. The older Citroens look like squashed roller skates, but this one was brand new and, as we requested, featured four doors and a hatchback where we could stow the bike in an emergency. (An emergency that didn't require stowing the bike *and* the luggage, because that would require a different vehicle, namely an eighteen-wheeler.)

The most notable characteristic of this car was its appearance. It is almost impossible to describe. Instead of the usual metal (or fiberglass) body, the sides of the car appeared to be made out of…rubber. You can create this effect for yourself with a quick trip to Target. Buy two big rubber bath mats and glue them to the sides of your car. That's what our rental car looked like!

Moving along, after a few days of cycling up and down the Austrian Alps, the next day's route called for a climb up an 18% grade. If you want to know how steep an 18% grade is, lean a ladder up against your house and ride a bicycle up to the roof.

It's steep.

So, with a certain amount of cajoling, I was able to convince Brad to take the day off and ride in the car with me while the other cyclists spent several painful hours wondering what the hell they'd signed up for.

The best part was, this was going to be the day we skirted   the border of Slovenia, which would mean another notch in my belt!   (If you are wondering if I notch my belt every time I travel to a new country, the answer is "no." Have you never heard of a metaphor?)

We hadn't gotten out of the hotel parking lot before I realized I'd made a big mistake. Being the bossy pants he is, Brad had insisted on driving, but he has a very bad driving habit. He refuses to exceed the speed limit. Ever.

When I yelled at him (as people passed us going twice as fast) he said, "Didn't you see that sign?"

What sign? The only sign I'd seen was one telling us we were on the road to Slovenia: SLO.

Ha ha, I said. Now step on it!

At some point, he casually announced that we wouldn't actually be driving *in* to Slovenia — just *up* to it. To the border checkpoint.

"What do you mean?" I asked.

He said, "Hertz told us in no uncertain terms that we cannot take the car into Slovenia."

"Yeah, so?   We'll just *barely* drive in, then we'll drive right back out!"

"No."

Well, this was just unacceptable.   Obviously, this meant I wouldn't be able to notch my belt (again, not a real belt.) "Why the hell not?" I demanded.   "Because Hertz said so, that's why."

We carried on like this, back and forth as we crept SLO-ly up the 18% grade until I realized I'd lost the argument.   To hear Brad tell it, Hertz was probably fearful that if you drove into the country, unknown Slovenians would run out of the woods and kill you and take your car, bathmats and all.

But that's just silly.   Nobody would want those stupid bathmats.

Sum Big Dumpling

I have never had any interest in being on a big ship for a prolonged period of time — what some people call "cruising."

There are a couple of reasons for this: first, I tend to get claustrophobic and you can't get off a ship, no matter how big it is, in the middle of the ocean. (Well, you can get off but you probably won't get back on.) Second, I detest buffets and I've been told that being on a cruise is just one endless buffet. Finally, I don't like the idea of getting tossed around a little cabin in a storm, or any other time for that matter. A little round window? No, thanks.

Also, I've never had any burning desire to see "Down Under," as in Australia and New Zealand. I don't mind making fun of their accents — "throw a shrimp on the barbie" and all that— but I'm not big on nature and I've heard enough about the snakes and spiders in both countries to know that it's way too much nature for me.

So, when our friends Greg and John invited us to accompany them on a cruise between Australia and New Zealand, it was an easy "no."

A few months later, they had to scrape me off the ship because I wanted to stay on it forever.

Let's just say that cruising was an entirely different experience than I'd expected.

First, there is the ship itself. Many large cruise ships hold as many as 6,000 passengers and 2,000 crew. The world's largest cruise ship has 18 decks and features a 10-story water slide! To move that many people around, say for dinner, would take a lot of elevators and waiting-for-elevators, so I can easily see why somebody would just jump on a water slide, tuxedo and all. But not me.

Ours was a sedate little ship that held 500 passengers and 400 crew. It was designed like a Four Seasons Hotel — elegant and sophisticated and not all brassy and glassy like some I've seen in photos.

Our cabin was like a suite in a very nice hotel and featured a dining table, large sofa, balcony and one of the nicest bathrooms (with double sinks) I've ever seen.

Now you see why they had to scrape me off that ship at the end of our 16-day cruise.

We flew to Sydney, Australia, to commence our journey and spent four days in the Four Seasons to "prepare" us for the ship. During that time we did the usual touristy things which included lots of walking around and people-watching. We also did a double-decker bus tour which you may have read about elsewhere in this book.

One day we decided to climb — yes, climb — the Sydney Harbour Bridge which turns out to be a real "thing."

Like many bridges, the Sydney Bridge consists of a flat surface on which cars, trains and people traverse the water, and two mammoth arched spans which hold the bridge up. That's the part we climbed: the big, curved arches, like climbing an enormous hill and then descending the other side. When you look down between your feet, you can see a level of cars and bicycles and under that a train, and under that, the ocean.

When we arrived for our scheduled climb, we were asked to wait in the gift shop which contained all the usual tourist crap (T-shirts, hats, post-cards, etc.) but it also contained a display of various V.I.P.-types who had come before us — people like Oprah, Daniel Radcliffe and the cast of Modern Family. I figured if Oprah could do it, I certainly could!

Safety is of paramount concern when climbing a bridge (apparently somebody gets yelled at if you fall off), so the people who manage the bridge insist that everybody follow strict safety protocols. First, we were all told to put on a two-tone, blue, adult "onesie" that made us look like the Teletubbies dressed for a moon mission. (The suit zipped up the front, just as my pants do, but I can't zip my pants up all the way to my chin.)

Next, we were each issued walkie-talkie type headsets so we could listen to the tour leader who apparently planned to talk to us throughout the climb. Finally, we were tethered to a cable that traversed the entire route so if our feet slipped off the metal beams at least we wouldn't fall to our deaths but, rather, would remain there, dangling in air by a little tiny thread of steel.

There were about twenty of us in our particular group, and after we climbed single-file to to the top of the bridge we were photographed and, miraculously, the photos were available for purchase in the gift shop when we returned to the starting place. Imagine!

(I'm being sarcastic. Of course we could buy photos. It would only be a miracle if they weren't. And I totally believe that their prohibition about taking your own cell phone is simply for our own safety. I'm sure it has nothing to do with preventing us from taking our own — free -- photos.)

Naturally, we bought the photo of us atop the bridge and I later posted it on Facebook, after which one of my friends asked, in all seriousness, "You look like twins. Do you always dress alike?"

(Yes, and we always wear walkie-talkie headsets. What's wrong with you anyway?)

In New Zealand — which features some of the most stunning scenery I have ever seen — we signed up for various off-ship excursions in the cities and towns where we docked. One of these was a visit to an actual Kiwi Farm where we were allowed to walk under an arbor-like structure from which thousands of plump, fuzzy green kiwis dangled.

A few days later we went on a "nature walk" (yes, you read that correctly) into a highly protected wildlife zone. Along the way the guide, who spoke what I assumed was English, pointed out various plants, flowers and trees and kept up a running commentary of what his country was doing to protect each one. I didn't pay a lot of attention to his lecture, believing that if I can eat it I will and if not, well, I don't really want to talk about it.

But at some point he stopped abruptly and said, "Shhhh! I think it might be a kiwi!"

I couldn't imagine what could possibly be so exciting about a kiwi since we had seen a million of them falling off the trees just a few days earlier, but we all stood while he pointed to a wooden shoebox-looking thing on the ground.

"Shhh!" he whispered. "I think it's in there!"

I was still fixated on the kiwi *fruit* of course, so I said to the guy next to me (who, fortunately, turned out to be Brad), "Let's eat it!"

As you've probably guessed by now, the New Zealanders are apparently running out of words so they call everything "kiwi" — whether it's a fuzzy piece of fruit or a feathered animal that sleeps in a wooden shoebox. It never budged the entire time we filed by silently, wide-eyed (well, some people were), and the tour guide held the lid of the box mid-air to allow us an unobstructed view.

As we continued down the trail Brad uttered one of his Bradisms to the great amusement of some of the others: "This gives me a great idea for the next fast-food craze: "Kiwi-in-a-Box!" Then he added, as if anybody needed an explanation, "Like Jack-in-the-Box."

Later, back on the ship, I decided I was now brave enough to venture into one of the hot tubs on board. I'm a bit self-conscious about my weight these days and didn't particularly want to soak with a big group of strangers, so I was delighted to find a completely empty hot tub on one of the forward decks. I made Brad race back to the room with me to change into our swimsuits, hoping we could get back and into the water before anybody else came around.

The tub was still empty when we got back, so I bravely threw off my towel and climbed up the steps to get in. I was so grateful that there wasn't anybody near by to see me.

As we settled into the hot water, I glanced around and

discovered, when I looked up, that we were directly below the bridge — the name of the control room where the Captain and his large and nosy staff steer the ship. And there they were, all of them, looking down intently at the two old men who were half-naked in the hot tub below. We would still be in that hot tub, too — I didn't want to prolong the show by climbing up and down that little ladder again — if Brad hadn't insisted I get out so we could go to dinner.

After his "Kiwi-in-a-Box" crack I'm surprised he didn't come up with something similar to describe the hot tub scene, something Chinese maybe, like, "Sum Big Dumpling."

Turning 70

We all want to feel special on our birthdays, right? I happen to believe that milestone birthdays — those divisible by "10" — are appropriate to celebrate. All others can be acknowledged — with a friendly phone call, email, or spoken "happy birthday" — but please, do not invite me to your 34th birthday party because I can tell you now: that's the day I'm having the dog washed.

My own milestone birthday parties began when I turned 30 and my wife gave me a surprise party. It was great fun and I was surrounded by the people I loved the most. It wasn't until the next day that I realized I was no longer in my twenties. I was officially "old" and wondered if I should start driving slow and stop using my turn signal.

You can imagine my surprise when, ten years later, I lived to see 40. I was no longer married and about to make the move of a lifetime — from my hometown of Denver, where I was born and raised and spent the past 40 years, to Houston, Texas, which would quickly become my adopted home and where I would spend the next 17 years.

My fortieth birthday party was another big surprise, hosted by one of my favorite people of all time, Liz. Liz knew everybody in town and everybody knew her, so it only stands to reason that she would throw my party at what was then known as Mile High Stadium — home of the Broncos. My birthday is in June, so the Broncos weren't playing, but the Denver Zephyrs baseball team was, so Liz and I and a hundred of our best friends occupied the owner's box where hot dogs and Champagne were served while we watched a Zephyrs game. The highlight of the party was when my name and photo appeared on the massive electronic scoreboard — the one and only time my name is likely to appear on a scoreboard during a sporting event.

My fiftieth birthday, ten years later, was to be in Paris. Several of my friends had flown over from Denver and Houston ahead of time, but my kids and I had to wait a few days so we could attend my son's high school graduation. We were expected to arrive in Paris the day before the big party hosted by two of my dearest French friends.

Even something as depressing as turning 50 can be tolerable if it does not include the singing of the song "Happy Birthday," which I detest — but wish I'd written if only for the $50 million in royalty checks it has generated. Think back to all the times you've sung Happy Birthday over the years. Did you know you were supposed to pay a royalty each time you did so? Me, neither. Fortunately, there probably wasn't anybody there from ASCAP to fine you, but if you want to voluntarily pay up, feel free to send me a check and I'll pass it on the the owner of the copyright. It's the least I can do.

Fortunately, the French haven't come up with a tune comparable to Happy Birthday. All they do is wish you a "Bon anniversaire," kiss you on both cheeks and hand you another glass of Champagne. Very civilized, and exactly why I chose Paris as the place to celebrate my 50th.

There was one glitch. Between Houston and Paris we had to change planes in Newark, New Jersey, where we discovered that Air France had just gone on strike and there wouldn't be any more flights to Paris. I knew on the spot that I would not spend my 50th birthday in Newark, New Jersey, so the kids and I decided to go to Acapulco instead. My friends all celebrated my birthday in Paris without me, while the kids and I celebrated in Mexico without them. Feliz cumpleaños!

My 60th also took place in France, and this time I was actually there. Brad was starting a bicycle trip and I was tagging along, so on June 1 we celebrated with one other couple in a little outdoor cafe in the idyllic village of Cordes-sur-Ciel in the south of France. It was nice, but the other couple celebrating with us were people we'd met on a previous trip to Mexico, so after the third bottle of Champagne, I didn't know if I should be saying "Bon anniversaire" or "Feliz cumpleaños."

(In proofreading this chapter, Brad pointed out that I shouldn't have been saying either one, since it was *my* birthday.)

My most recent milestone birthday was the "Big Seven-Oh" as I've taken to calling it (because that's the kind of thing 70-year-olds get by with) — and was strictly a family affair, at my request. We found a location which was within easy driving distance of my kids, who live in Nashville and New York City. This turned out to be right smack in the middle of the woods of West Virginia. (Or "West Virginny" as some locals call it.)

I'd never been to West Virginia before — or North, South or East Virginia either, for that matter, so I was unprepared for how beautiful it is. When you think of rolling green hills and broad verdant valleys, you're thinking of West Virginia.

Lest you assume we chose a tarpaper shack out in the wild, I should mention that we holed up at The Greenbrier resort, which one of my friends described as "similar to a Four Seasons hotel — if the Four Seasons were run by hillbillies."

We didn't find that to be true, although one waiter did tell us a disturbing story about his living situation which involved the chickens living inside and outside his house.

When I just asked Brad to confirm this story to make sure I was remembering it correctly, he said, "Well, we have chickens inside our house, too." I looked at him quizzically and he added, "Ours just live in the freezer." This is what I put up with.

The Greenbrier is, in fact, everything you imagine when you think of "Southern splendor," assuming you ever think of "Southern splendor." It has over 700 guest rooms in a maze of stately white buildings in the middle of 11,000 acres of land. It's been in business since 1778, and 27 Presidents have stayed there. It is, we discovered, a National Historic Landmark and is affectionately known as "America's Resort."

Oh, and did I mention that there is a strict dress code? This blast from the past ("Southern splendor") states, among other things, that "hats are not allowed to be worn in the dining room, but bonnets are always in style for the ladies."

I don't know what "ladies" the Greenbrier has been hanging out with, but I seriously doubted that any of the five females in my family would be wearing "bonnets." And it turned out I was right.

Don't get me wrong. We loved every minute of our time at The Greenbrier. We had arranged to be lodged in a "cottage" consisting of four bedrooms and baths, so each couple had their own suite and the three granddaughters had one to share. We had a living room and dining room, but no kitchen. Rather, food was brought to us, or if we were feeling particularly energetic, we could don our bonnets and walk a few yards to the hotel and eat in one of its many restaurants.

For me, the highlight of those four days, aside from being surrounded by my family, was the gift of a lifetime: a large, beautifully bound book containing thoughtful and heartwarming letters from each of my children and grandchildren as well as a large sampling of notes from life-long friends. As you might expect, it is one of my most treasured possessions. Never mind that the cover features a photo of a three-year old Rex John dressed in what can only be described as a frightful little farmer's outfit: big overalls with the cuffs turned up about three inches and a plaid wool cap with ear flaps. I look goofy.

Apparently my children have inherited the humor gene.

The cottage also had a spacious veranda with rocking chairs, presumably so I could practice being 70. One afternoon there was a lull in the family hubbub, so I warily sat down in one and found I liked it. I tried rocking just a little as I enjoyed the peaceful landscape spread out before me.

After a few minutes my youngest granddaughter came

out of the cottage and sat down in the rocker beside me. "Gampy," she said, "tell me a story." And because she's quite precocious for her tender age, she added, "And try to make it funny."

"I'll do my best, sweet girl," I said.

Acknowledgments

When you watch the Academy Awards, have you ever noticed how some blabbermouth always goes on and on until the orchestra starts playing louder and louder to try to give him a hint that his time is up?

Well strike up the band folks, because I have a lot of people to thank for the little book you now hold in your hands.

First, and most obviously, there is my *Main Victim*: Brad. Bradley. The Bradster. Thanks, Speedo, for allowing me to use you as my foil, to ever so slightly exaggerate the amusing things you say and do all day, every day. If you go back through this book and take out the chapters where you *aren't* mentioned, it would be a very thin book indeed.

Then, there are the other seven people who are in my head and heart 24/7: Elisabeth, Jonathan, Bill, Kelly, Abigail, Alexis, Ava. Thanks, family, for always being there for me.

This book is filled with people who have wittingly or unwittingly given me material. The ones who have said or done something outrageous are mentioned by pseudonyms. A few are mentioned by first name only: Cara, Carol, Christine, Greg and John, "Jill," Liz, Lois, "Bill and Polly," Doug and Brenda, Nick, Nicole, Teresa, and my cousins Donna and Linda. Those in quotes have been given pseudonyms — to protect their anonymity.

My pen-pals' names are real, and I really would love to hear from them: Mizue Aoki, Daniel Vanlangenaker and Elisabeth Bayer.

Other people aren't mentioned by name, but they are an integral part of one of the stories: Dave and Joan, Chuck and Ramona, Michel and Didier.

For each of my books I depend on a select group of special friends who serve as advance readers to help me get to a final, final draft. If they don't like something, it goes in the trash. If they make a suggestion, nine times out of ten, I take it. For this book this special group included Don Bell and Jan Bergman, Arvella Dobaran, Norma Gandy, Lois and Les Reese, Dick and Jody Ridgeway, and Bonnie and Bruce Shively. Thank you dear friends, for your invaluable help.

Another group of especially important people in my life are: Susan, Angie, Allan & Cynthia, Esther and Terry, Rico and Maya, Jan and Bill, Mac and Betha, John & Linda, Jim & Leslie and Peggy. *Thank you!*

Finally, my life is jam-packed with people who make me laugh and smile on a regular basis. Some of these people go back 60 years; others just arrived. For all of them, I am forever grateful.

Laughter is the shortest distance between two people. - Victor Borge

You may also enjoy these other works by Rex John

Makeovers - Carson Kirkpatrick doesn't like the way the world is going. People are lazy and stupid. Worse, they are unkempt and bad-mannered. Something must be done and he -- born to power and privilege -- is just the person to do it.

> *"I recommend this thriller to anyone who enjoys their crime fiction with a touch of humor." - G.S., Lakewood, CO*
>
> *"An expected pleasure...an enticing, canny and interesting read...leaves the reader wanting more." - J.P., Houston, TX*
>
> *"Just the right touches of intrigue, humor, and thoughtful character development." - S.L., Denver, CO*
>
> *"Makeovers held me from the first page to the last." - T.P., Boise, ID*

The Pillow Goes Under Your Head - When author Rex John says "life is funny," he should know -- and these 34 short stories from his own life prove it. To say his parents dressed him funny as a child is an understatement, but his choices as an adult weren't much better -- from the time he wore a Mexican sombrero to a black-tie event to the time he dressed as Mrs. Doubtfire for a Halloween party. Some people enjoy the great outdoors, but this author certainly doesn't -- and who can blame him? His various attempts to become "one with nature" always end badly, from his winter camp-outs as a Boy Scout to his encounters with a baboon in South Africa and pigs on the island of Corsica. And don't even think about asking him to get on a horse. This was the author's second book -- but his first attempt at humor.

The Flying Shoe - Trevor is new to Portland and needs to make friends. When he meets Sean, Amy, and Nate -- scruffy street kids who hang out at a local coffee shop -- he makes an effort to befriend them. Sean is full of attitude, but he needs Trevor's help to solve a problem that involves five dollars, a death, and a "borrowed" car.

"A great, short read!" - C.H., Huntsville, TX
"Engaging! That's all I will say because I don't want to give away the end." - H.H., Denver, CO
"Friendship, loneliness and guilt. Touching and thought-provoking. Highly recommended! - L.G., via Amazon.com

Available at **Amazon.com** or by request from your local bookstore.

23073128R00122

Made in the USA
San Bernardino, CA
20 January 2019